Haydn Richards
Junior English 4

Acknowledgements

Grateful acknowledgement is made to the following for permission to use copyright material:

page 6 **Attacked by a crow**
Watership Down by Richard Adams.
By kind permission of Rex Collings Ltd.

12 **Toad and company**
The Wind in the Willows by Kenneth Grahame.
By kind permission of Methuen & Co. Ltd., and of the University Chest, Oxford, the owner of the copyright.

24 **Rikki-tikki and Darzee**
The Jungle Book by Rudyard Kipling.
By kind permission of the National Trust, Macmillan London Ltd., and Doubleday & Co. Inc.

48 **Inside the vault**
The Ghost of Thomas Kempe by Penelope Lively.
By kind permission of William Heinemann Ltd.

54 **A pony for Jody**
The Red Pony by John Steinbeck.
By kind permission of William Heinemann Ltd.

60 **Encounter with a dinosaur**
Originally appeared in Saturday Evening Post as *The Beast From 20,000 Fathoms*. Copyright © 1951 by Ray Bradbury, renewed 1978 by Ray Bradbury. Reprinted by permission of the Harold Matson Company, Inc.

66 **Tarka fights Deadlock**
Tarka the Otter by Henry Williamson.
By kind permission of The Bodley Head Ltd.

84 **A fight in a signal tower**
The Eagle of the Ninth by Rosemary Sutcliff.
By kind permission of Oxford University Press.

Designed by Michael Soderberg

Illustrated by Barry Rowe, Martin White
Beverly Curl, David Atkinson and Caroline Bilson

© Haydn Richards 1965
Revised edition 1997
EOU Printing 2002

ISBN 0 602 22547 7

Published by Ginn and Company
Linacre House, Jordan Hill,
Oxford OX2 8DP
A part of Harcourt Education Ltd.

Ginn on the Internet http://www.ginn.co.uk
Filmset by Wyvern Typesetting Ltd, Bristol

Printed and Bound at Multivista Global Ltd, Chennai-600 042, India

Preface

The main aim of Haydn Richards Junior English is to enable the pupil to work alone, as far as is possible. For this reason complete lists of the words needed to answer the various exercises are given. Being thus provided with the necessary tools, the pupil should experience little difficulty in doing the work.

The course provides ample and varied practice in all the English topics usually taught in the Junior School. Such simple grammatical terms as are essential to the understanding of the language are introduced at appropriate stages, together with simple definitions, lucid explanations and easy examples.

The meaning of every proverb and idiom dealt with is given, so that these may be used correctly in both writing and conversation.

A noteworthy feature of each book in the series is the detailed alphabetical Contents, facilitating reference to any particular topic by the teacher and the older pupils.

In addition to teaching and testing such topics as Parts of Speech, Opposites, Synonyms, Homophones, Punctuation, Direct and Indirect Speech, Sentence Linkage and Structure, etc., the course includes verbal intelligence exercises designed to stimulate clear thinking, so that by the end of the fourth year the pupil who has worked steadily through the course is well equipped for any entrance examination.

H.R.

Contents

Nouns

The **butcher** gave the **dog** a big meaty **bone**.

butcher is the name of a **person**.
dog is the name of an **animal**.
bone is the name of a **thing**.

A noun is the name of a person, animal or thing.

A Make a list of the nouns shown in this picture.

B Find the nouns in these sentences and write them down.

1 The car skidded on the ice and hit a tree.

2 Diamonds, rubies and emeralds are precious stones.

3 There are eleven players in a soccer team.

4 A dog is sometimes called 'man's best friend'.

5 The chief city of a country is called the capital.

6 The heart pumps blood to the body.

7 Rust is caused by oxygen in the air.

8 The referee ordered the offending player off the field.

C Complete the nouns with missing letters.

1 A r _ _ _ _ _ _ _ _ is a place where you can buy and eat a meal.

2 A h _ _ _ _ _ _ _ _ is a kind of plane capable of rising straight up from the ground and hovering in the air.

3 An artist mixes his colours on a p _ _ _ _ _ _ .

4 A tr _ _ _ _ _ _ has three sides and three angles.

5 A d _ _ _ _ _ is a coin or banknote used in the United States of America and other countries.

1

Verbs

Mother **swept** the floor and **polished** it.

The words **swept** and **polished** are doing words or verbs.

A verb is a word which shows action.

ACORN ST

A Make a list of the verbs in these sentences.

1 Fish breathe through their gills.

2 Many animals hibernate during the winter.

3 Some of them wake and search for food on mild days.

4 After digging the garden, Father raked it well.

5 Brazil produces and exports vast quantities of coffee.

6 The ship struck an iceberg and sank.

B Copy the verbs in the column on the left, then opposite each write the meaning from the list below which matches it.

apologize	1	to breathe in
bewilder	2	to eat like an animal
comprehend	3	to become less stiff or firm
confess	4	to tell as a secret
confide	5	to spend the winter asleep
demolish	6	to uncover; to lay open
devour	7	to express regret
discuss	8	to put out; to wipe out
expose	9	to work hard or try hard
extinguish	10	to understand
fortify	11	to make strong
glare	12	to pull or tear down
hibernate	13	to annoy; to irritate
inhale	14	to stare in anger
loathe	15	to confuse completely
meditate	16	to think quietly
pester	17	to own up to a sin
relax	18	to join together
strive	19	to talk over
unite	20	to regard with disgust

2

Adjectives

The captain had a **black bushy** beard.

The words **black** and **bushy** describe the captain's beard.

A word which describes a noun is called an adjective.

A Make a list of the adjectives in these sentences.

1 Rabbits become tame and affectionate when kept as pets.

2 Fruit for jam-making must be sound, ripe, dry and clean.

3 The Canadian prairies are vast plains where huge quantities of wheat are grown.

4 Tame mice are sociable but quarrelsome creatures.

5 The otter has short legs, webbed toes and thick fur.

6 To withstand rough winds, lighthouses are built of interlocking blocks of masonry.

B Copy the adjectives in the column on the left. Opposite each write the meaning from the list below which matches it.

arrogant	1 richly coloured; splendid
boisterous	2 giving a warm welcome
contemptuous	3 very scornful
distinguished	4 requiring much work
elaborate	5 boastfully proud
frantic	6 successful; thriving
gorgeous	7 well-known; famous
hospitable	8 heavy and clumsy
intelligent	9 bright; shining
laborious	10 quick at learning
memorable	11 self-important
obstinate	12 not moving
pompous	13 very noisy and disorderly
ponderous	14 worked out with great care
prosperous	15 not running or flowing
radiant	16 stubborn
repulsive	17 rough; violent
stagnant	18 causing strong dislike
stationary	19 not to be forgotten
tumultuous	20 wild with rage or pain

Adverbs

1 The troops fought **gallantly**.

Gallantly tells **how** the troops fought. (*manner*)

2 We looked **everywhere** for the lost ball.

Everywhere tells **where** we looked. (*place*)

3 We looked for the lost ball **yesterday**.

Yesterday tells **when** we looked. (*time*)

A word which describes how, where or when an action is performed is called an adverb.

A Make a list of the adverbs in these sentences. After each write **how**, **where** or **when** as required.

1 Nigel washed the dishes carefully.

2 Diana calls to see us frequently.

3 All the rabbits ran away.

4 The two boys wandered aimlessly round the town.

5 The train will be arriving shortly.

6 Dozens of rooks were cawing noisily.

B Complete each sentence by using a suitable adverb from the column on the left.

awkwardly	1 The thief struggled ____ .
bitterly	2 We waited ____ .
contentedly	3 The robin chirped ____ .
courageously	4 The child wept ____ .
distinctly	5 The old man fell ____ .
frugally	6 The champion fought ____ .
gracefully	7 The miser lives ____ .
hungrily	8 He ate his food ____ .
intimately	9 The cows grazed ____ .
merrily	10 He raised his hat ____ .
mournfully	11 The wind howled ____ .
patiently	12 We all laughed ____ .
politely	13 The girls danced ____ .
soundly	14 The baby slept ____ .
uproariously	15 He speaks ____ .
violently	16 I know him ____ .

Nouns number

Singular	Plural
chief	chiefs
chimney	chimneys
deer	deer
diary	diaries
Eskimo	Eskimos
factory	factories
goose	geese
hero	heroes
man	men
mouse	mice
ox	oxen
photo	photos
piano	pianos
potato	potatoes
sheaf	sheaves
shelf	shelves
son-in-law	sons-in-law
thief	thieves
turkey	turkeys
wolf	wolves

A Write the plurals of these words.

1 piano
2 sheaf
3 chimney
4 hero
5 mouse
6 diary
7 goose
8 photo
9 thief
10 chief
11 deer
12 Eskimo
13 factory
14 son-in-law
15 man

B Write the missing words.

1 factory — many ___
2 turkey — a flock of ___
3 chief — two ___
4 potato — a sack of ___
5 thief — a gang of ___
6 wolf — a pack of ___
7 piano — four ___
8 deer — a herd of ___
9 ox — a team of ___
10 mouse — three ___

C Rewrite these sentences, changing the nouns in bold type to the plural number and making any other changes which may be necessary.

1 The **thief** removed the **turkey** from the **shelf**.

2 The **Eskimo** was armed with a long **knife**.

3 The **hero** had his **photo** taken.

4 The **child** looked at the little white **mouse**.

5 The **fox** looked longingly at the **goose**.

Attacked by a crow

Silver was almost at the crest when suddenly, from half-way up, there came a high screaming – the sound a rabbit makes, not to call for help or frighten the enemy, but simply out of terror. Fiver and Pipkin, limping behind the others, and conspicuously undersized and tired, were being attacked by the crow. It had flown low along the ground. Then, pouncing, it had aimed a blow of its great bill at Fiver, who just managed to dodge in time. Now it was leaping and hopping among the grass tussocks, striking at the two rabbits with terrible darts of its head. Crows aim at the eyes and Pipkin, sensing this, had buried his head in a clump of rank grass and was trying to burrow farther in. It was he who was screaming.

Hazel covered the distance down the slope in a few seconds. He had no idea what he was going to do and if the crow had ignored him he would probably have been at a loss. But by dashing he distracted its attention and it turned on him. He swerved past it, stopped and, looking back, saw Bigwig come racing in from the opposite side. The crow turned again, struck at Bigwig and missed. Hazel heard its beak hit a pebble in the grass with a sound like a snail-shell when a thrush beats it on a stone. As Silver followed Bigwig, it recovered itself and faced him squarely. Silver stopped short in fear and the crow seemed to dance before him, its great, black wings flapping in a horrible commotion. It was just about to stab when Bigwig ran straight into it from behind and knocked it sideways . . .

Watership Down   Richard Adams

1   Where was Silver when he heard the screaming?
2   Why was Pipkin screaming in this way?
3   Why had the crow chosen Pipkin and Fiver for attack?
4   With what did the crow aim at Fiver?
5   How did Pipkin attempt to escape the crow's attack?
6   Who ran to Pipkin's aid?
7   In what way did this action assist Pipkin?
8   To what does the writer compare the sound made by the crow's beak on the pebble?
9   Which two creatures stood face to face in this fight?
10 What stopped the crow from stabbing at Silver?

Alphabetical order

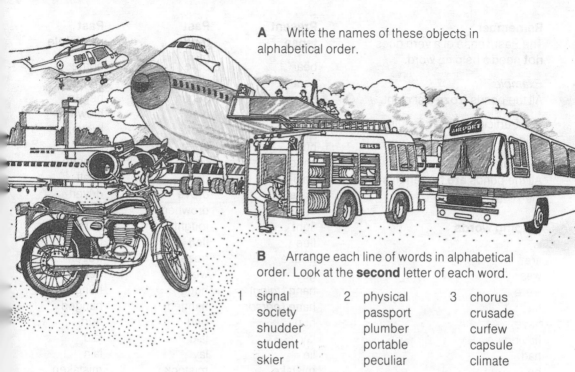

A Write the names of these objects in alphabetical order.

B Arrange each line of words in alphabetical order. Look at the **second** letter of each word.

1 signal
   society
   shudder
   student
   skier

2 physical
   passport
   plumber
   portable
   peculiar

3 chorus
   crusade
   curfew
   capsule
   climate

C Look at the **third** letter of each word when arranging them in alphabetical order.

1 blizzard
   blunder
   blockade
   bladder
   bleak

2 ground
   granite
   gruesome
   grease
   gristle

3 splint
   sparrow
   sprawl
   spectre
   spiral

Look at these words:
hear; **hea**p; **hea**t; **hea**d; **hea**l

Notice that the **first three letters** of each word are the same – **hea**.

To arrange these words in alphabetical order, we must look at the **fourth** letter of each.

These are:
r p t d l

Letters in alphabetical order:
d l p r t

Words in alphabetical order:
hea**d** hea**l** hea**p** hea**r** hea**t**

D Arrange in alphabetical order, looking at the **fourth** letter.

catkin
cattle
catch
catalogue
catgut

2 promise
   profit
   produce
   problem
   proceed

3 sprout
   spruce
   sprint
   spray
   spread

retreat
return
retail
retort
retire

5 patriot
   patch
   pattern
   patent
   patient

Verbs past tense and participle

Remember
The Past Tense of a verb does **not** need a helping word.

Example
All the ponds **froze** last night.

The Participle always requires a helping word.

Example
All the ponds **are frozen** this morning.

Helping words
is
are
was
were
has
have
having
had
be
been
being
am

Present tense	Past tense	Past participle
bear	bore	borne
beat	beat	beaten
begin	began	begun
blow	blew	blown
break	broke	broken
burst	burst	burst
choose	chose	chosen
deal	dealt	dealt
drive	drove	driven
drown	drowned	drowned
fight	fought	fought
flee	fled	fled
freeze	froze	frozen
go	went	gone
hang (*thing*)	hung	hung
hang (*person*)	hanged	hanged
hurt	hurt	hurt
lay	laid	laid
lie	lay	lain
mistake	mistook	mistaken
show	showed	shown
slay	slew	slain
think	thought	thought
weave	wove	woven
wring	wrung	wrung

A   In each sentence below insert the **past tense** of the verb in bold type.

1   Tom and John _____ a gruelling fight.   **fight**

2   The defeated army _____ before their pursuers.   **flee**

3   The gladiator _____ his opponent with his sword.   **slay**

4   On reaching home Veronica _____ the table for tea.   **lay**

5   Dad _____ his hand with an electric drill.   **hurt**

6   The spider _____ a web in a very short time.   **weave**

7 His teacher ____ him for his twin brother. **mistake**

8 Vast floods ____ hundreds of sheep yesterday. **drown**

B Copy each sentence and complete by inserting the **past participle** of the verb in bold type.

1 We rested after our visitors had ____. **go**

2 He had ____ of a good answer to the question. **think**

3 Several passengers were ____ in the collision. **hurt**

4 David was ____ to captain the school team. **choose**

5 This lovely scarf was ____ by hand. **weave**

6 The condemned man was ____ at eight o'clock in the morning. **hang**

7 Margaret did the sum after her teacher had ____ her the right method. **show**

8 The ground was ____ so the match was postponed. **freeze**

C Insert in each space either the **past tense** or the **past participle** of the verb in bold type, as required.

1 The patient ____ the pain without flinching. **bear**

2 The old ship is to be ____ up next month. **break**

3 Many trees were ____ down during the gale. **blow**

4 Work was ____ on the new school yesterday. **begin**

5 The winner ____ the racing car skilfully. **drive**

6 Our team will probably be ____ in the final. **beat**

7 After lunch Grandma ____ down to rest. **lie**

8 Barbara washed the towel and ____ it out. **wring**

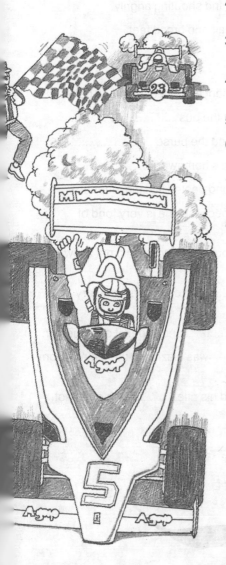

9

Sentences and phrases

Look at this group of words.
Mr. Dobbin bought a new sports car yesterday.

Does it make sense? Yes.
Does it contain a verb? Yes.

Then it is a **sentence**.

A sentence is a group of words which make sense. Every sentence contains a verb.

Look at this group of words.
Without even a glance at his book

Does it make sense? No.
Does it contain a verb? No.

Then it is not a sentence; it is a **phrase**.

A Say whether each group of words is a sentence or a phrase.

1 Most trees shed their leaves every autumn.

2 Early in the autumn of every year

3 The majority of men throughout the entire world

4 Most people work.

5 The farmer chased the boys.

6 Waving his stick and shouting angrily.

7 Dogs with long hair and broad feet

8 Dogs bark.

B Form a sentence from each phrase below.

1 Whilst waiting for the bus ....

2 The boy who found the purse ....

3 Having finished his homework ....

4 .... and posted it in the letter box.

5 .... because she is very fond of chocolates.

6 .... but the doctor would not allow him to get up.

7 The milkman .... on our doorstep every morning.

8 The goalkeeper .... and tipped it over the bar.

9 A huge fire .... was blazing in the dining-room grate.

10 The hunter raised his rifle .... with one shot.

Nouns gender

Masculine	Feminine
bachelor	spinster
boar	sow
buck	doe
bull	cow
conductor	conductress
drake	duck
emperor	empress
heir	heiress
host	hostess
lord	lady
marquis	marchioness
mayor	mayoress
nephew	niece
peacock	peahen
proprietor	proprietress
ram	ewe
sir	madam
stag	hind
widower	widow
wizard	witch

A   Write the **feminine** gender of:

1   sir
2   bachelor
3   lord
4   mayor
5   peacock
6   emperor
7   marquis
8   bullock
9   nephew
10   heir

B   Write the **masculine** gender of:

1   duck
2   sow
3   widow
4   witch
5   hind
6   hostess
7   niece
8   ewe
9   doe
10   empress

C   In each sentence change the **masculine** noun to the **feminine** gender.

1   The proprietor of the guest house welcomed every guest.

2   A beautiful peacock strutted about the lawn.

3   The conductor rang the bell and the bus started.

4   He sent a handsome present to his nephew.

5   The marquis is cruising in the Mediterranean.

6   The letter began, Dear Sir.

D   Complete each sentence by using a noun of the opposite gender to that in bold type.

1   Farmer Bond keeps ten pigs, two **boars** and eight ____ .

2   The **drake** swam on the pond while the ____ waddled round the farmyard with her little ones.

3   A record price was paid for the ____ and the **cow**.

4   **Lord** and ____ Bryce were at the garden party.

5   The wool on the **ram** was thicker than that on the ____ .

6   The red deer **stag** had antlers; the ____ had none.

11

Toad and company

When they were quite ready the now triumphant Toad led his companions to the paddock and set them to capture the old grey horse, who, without having been consulted, and to his own extreme annoyance, had been told off by Toad for the dustiest job in this dusty expedition. He frankly preferred the paddock, and took a great deal of catching. Meantime Toad packed the lockers still tighter with necessaries, and hung nose-bags, nets of onions, bundles of hay, and baskets from the bottom of the cart. At last the horse was caught and harnessed, and they set off, all talking at once, each animal either trudging by the side of the cart or sitting on the shaft, as the humour took him. It was a golden afternoon. The smell of the dust they kicked up was rich and satisfying; out of thick orchards on either side of the road birds called and whistled to them cheerily; good-natured wayfarers, passing them, gave them "Good day," or stopped to say nice things about their beautiful cart; and rabbits, sitting at their front doors in the hedgerows, held up their fore-paws and said, "O my! O my! O my!"

Late in the evening, tired and happy and miles from home, they drew up on a remote common far from habitations, turned the horse loose to graze, and ate their simple supper sitting on the grass by the side of the cart.

The Wind in the Willows   Kenneth Grahame

1 What did Toad set his companions to do?
2 Why did the old grey horse take a good deal of catching?
3 What did Toad hang from the bottom of the cart?
4 What were the animals doing when they were not trudging by the side of the cart?
5 How did the birds in the orchards greet the travellers?
6 What did the wayfarers say when they passed the travellers?
7 What did these people say when they stopped to talk to them?
8 Where did Toad and Company draw up late that evening?
9 What did they do with the horse?
10 Where did they eat their supper?

Nouns formation

Verb	Noun
abolish	abolition
accuse	accusation
acquaint	acquaintance
advertise	advertisement
advise	advice
applaud	applause
choose	choice
complain	complaint
complete	completion
converse	conversation
deceive	deceit
decide	decision
destroy	destruction
explain	explanation
explode	explosion
imagine	imagination
inquire	inquiry
pronounce	pronunciation
pursue	pursuit
satisfy	satisfaction

A Copy these phrases, inserting in the spaces the nouns formed from the verbs in bold type.

1 a lively _____ **imagine**
2 sound _____ **advise**
3 a violent _____ **explode**
4 widespread _____ **destroy**
5 a long _____ **converse**
6 a full-page _____ **advertise**
7 loud _____ **applaud**
8 correct _____ **pronounce**
9 a false _____ **accuse**
10 a serious _____ **complain**

B Complete each sentence by inserting the noun formed from the verb in bold type.

1 Purchasers have a _____ of several colours. **choose**

2 In 1833 an Act was passed for the _____ of slavery in the British Empire. **abolish**

3 Any _____ to increase pensions will be welcomed. **decide**

4 He listened patiently to his teacher's _____ . **explain**

5 The work was done to the customer's _____ . **satisfy**

6 Several hunters went in _____ of the lion. **pursue**

7 An _____ is a search for truth, knowledge or information. **inquire**

8 The work on the new road is nearing _____ . **complete**

9 _____ means making a person believe to be true something which is false. **deceive**

10 He is not really a friend, just an _____ . **acquaint**

13

Adjectives formation

Some adjectives are formed simply by adding the letter **y** to a noun.

Examples   cloud   cloudy
              mould   mouldy
              marsh   marshy

When the noun ends with **e**, this letter is dropped before the **y** is added.

Examples   shade   shady
              smoke   smoky
              juice   juicy

When **y** is added to some nouns the last letter is doubled.

Examples   sun   sunny
              mud   muddy
              star   starry

A   Use the adjective formed from the noun in bold type to fill each space. Copy the phrases in your book.

1   A material covered with **fluff**   a _____ material
2   A voice with a **squeak**   a _____ voice
3   Foods containing much **starch**   _____ foods
4   A man of great **wealth**   a _____ man
5   A morning with much **frost**   a _____ morning

B   Insert in each space the adjective formed from the noun in bold type. Remember to drop the final **e**.

1   A path with many **stones**   a _____ path
2   Hair in which there is a **wave**   _____ hair
3   Dishes covered with **grease**   _____ dishes
4   A day when a **breeze** is blowing a _____ day
5   A dinner with a nice **taste**   a _____ dinner
6   A beach covered with **pebbles**   a _____ beach

C   Form the adjective from the noun in bold type to fill each space. Remember to double the final letter.

1   An animal covered with **fur**   a _____ animal
2   A sound like that of **tin**   a _____ sound
3   Wood full of **knots**   _____ wood
4   Land which is largely **bog**   _____ land
5   A speech containing much **wit**   a _____ speech
6   A hand which is more **skin** than flesh a _____ hand

14

Direct speech

When we write the words spoken by someone we put **speech marks** round them. These are also called **inverted commas**.

Examples

"Please shut the door after you," said Rodney irritably.

The farmer shouted angrily, "Get out of that hayfield."

"If you don't work hard," said the teacher, "you will never succeed."

Notice how **"** is used at the beginning of the words spoken and **"** at the end.

A Copy these sentences and put speech marks round the words actually spoken.

1 Your shoelace is undone, Barbara, said Wendy.

2 Did you remember to bring a loaf, Sonia? asked her mother.

3 These cauliflowers were cut this morning, madam, said the greengrocer.

4 Keep him in bed for a few days, advised the doctor.

B Copy these sentences, putting speech marks where required.

1 The dentist said, you should have that tooth filled.

2 Linda remarked, this is the tastiest meal I have had for a long time.

3 Handing him ten pence the old lady said, thank you for your help, my boy.

4 The auctioneer asked, is there any advance on fifty pounds?

C Copy these sentences and put speech marks round the words actually spoken.

1 Please sir, said Oliver Twist to the master I want some more.

2 Oh, dear, sighed the old lady, I have lost the key of the house.

3 You will have to hurry, Mary, exclaimed her mother, or you will be late for school.

4 Stand to attention, shouted the sergeant, and hold your heads up.

Other words for said and asked

Using **said** or **asked** too often makes a composition monotonous.

Choose the most suitable word from the list on the left to complete each sentence.

A

admitted
announced
boasted
remarked
shouted
stammered
urged
whispered

1 "It is much colder today than it was yesterday," _____ the old boatman.

2 "Hush, Pamela," _____ her mother, "or you will wake the baby."

3 "Go on, Tony," _____ his teacher, "try to beat David's jump."

4 "All hands on deck," _____ the skipper of the trawler.

5 "I b-b-beg your pardon," _____ the frightened boy.

6 "Yes, it was I who broke the basin," _____ Carol.

7 "I am easily the best reader in the class," _____ Alan.

8 "The school will be closed all next week," _____ the headmaster.

B

coaxed
complained
grumbled
inquired
ordered
prophesied
protested
replied

1 "Prepare the theatre for an emergency operation at once," _____ the surgeon.

2 "Is this the way to the Post Office, please?" _____ the stranger.

3 "Yes," _____ the policeman, "keep straight on for about fifty metres and you will see it on your left."

4 "Please, Mummy, may I have just one more chocolate?" _____ Elizabeth.

5 "Your prices are far too high," _____ the customer to the grocer.

6 "I think we are going to have a very warm summer this year," _____ Aunt Jane.

7 "Your dog has been worrying my sheep, Mr. Bath," _____ the farmer.

8 "I get all the tedious jobs," _____ the shop assistant.

16

Collective nouns

actors	company
angels	host
arrows	sheaf; quiver
bells	peal
chicks	brood
directors	board
eggs	clutch
lions	pride
locusts	plague; swarm
magistrates	bench
minstrels	troupe
pilgrims	band
thieves	gang
singers	choir
spectators	crowd
stars	cluster
swallows	flight
teachers	staff
trees	clump
worshippers	congregation

Write the missing words.

A

1 a ＿＿ of singers
2 a ＿＿ of teachers
3 a ＿＿ of chicks
4 a ＿＿ of bells
5 a ＿＿ of actors
6 a ＿＿ of locusts
7 a ＿＿ of spectators
8 a ＿＿ of thieves
9 a ＿＿ of lions
10 a ＿＿ of swallows

B

1 a host of ＿＿
2 a clump of ＿＿
3 a cluster of ＿＿
4 a band of ＿＿
5 a board of ＿＿
6 a troupe of ＿＿
7 a quiver of ＿＿
8 a bench of ＿＿
9 a congregation of ＿＿
10 a clutch of ＿＿

C Write the collective nouns needed to complete these sentences.

1 The ＿＿ of pilgrims halted before the mosque.

2 A ＿＿ of locusts devoured every growing plant .

3 The mother hen was accompanied by her ＿＿ of chicks.

4 Under a small ＿＿ of trees a tent had been pitched.

5 Several plays have been performed by this brilliant ＿＿ of actors.

6 The police are searching for a ＿＿ of car thieves.

7 The ＿＿ of directors met to consider their company's losses.

8 The match was watched by a huge ＿＿ of spectators.

9 In his dream Jacob saw a ＿＿ of angels.

10 The children saw a ＿＿ of swallows making for the sea.

Wildlife in danger

It is a disturbing fact that today many different kinds of wild animal throughout the world are in danger of extinction. The reasons for this are many and varied, but we must largely blame pollution, pesticides, the disturbance of the animals' natural environment and man's greed and thoughtlessness.

Industry has grown enormously, and it has become common practice for factories to dispose of waste matter in streams and rivers, causing great loss of river life. Modern agricultural methods include the use of pesticides which effectively control insects classified as pests, but which also destroy many that are not. An increase in population has meant more building – and with it the destruction of much of the countryside that provides habitat for wild animals. To satisfy man's selfish desires the polar bear in North America is under threat, hunted by sportsmen; in Borneo and Sumatra the orang-utan has become part of a smuggling racket; in South America the chinchilla is almost extinct because its fur is in demand; whales are massacred world-wide for the oil and food they yield. These are only a few of the species under threat.

But the problem is receiving world-wide recognition, and some action is being taken. To name a few examples – sewage pollution in the River Thames has been greatly reduced; a ban on trading in some furs has been agreed; and organisations like Friends of the Earth do valuable work in this deserving cause.

1 Give in your own words two reasons why some species of wild animal may become extinct.
2 Why has it become common practice for factories to pollute streams and rivers?
3 Which insects are intended to be destroyed by pesticides?
4 What has brought about the destruction of much of the countryside?
5 Why is the polar bear in North America under threat?
6 Which countries have problems with smuggling?
7 Which animal is hunted for its fur?
8 Why are whales hunted in such large numbers?
9 What is being done to help preserve our river life?
10 Name one other way in which wild life is currently helped.

Fun with words

a _ _ _ _   a male farm animal

b _ _ _ _ _ _   a missile fired from a rifle

Word (**a**) is bull

Word (**b**) is bullet

Now try the exercise below. Remember that each dash stands for a letter, and that the second word of each pair is formed by adding letters to the first word.

A

1   **a** _ _ _ _   a large stringed instrument
    b _ _ _ _ _ _ _ _   a spear used in hunting whales

2   **a** _ _ _ _   a man who lives in a monastery
    b _ _ _ _ _ _   an agile and mischievous animal

3   **a** _ _ _   a young goat
    b _ _ _ _ _ _   to steal a person by force

4   **a** _ _ _   an article of headgear
    b _ _ _ _ _ _ _   a small axe

5   **a** _ _ _ _   an American coin of small value
    b _ _ _ _ _ _   the middle

6   **a** _ _ _ _   a place where ships can shelter
    b _ _ _ _ _ _ _ _   a part or a share

7   **a** _ _ _ _   stop
    b _ _ _ _ _ _   a rope or strap for leading an animal

8   **a** _ _ _ _   a man who entertains guests
    b _ _ _ _ _ _ _   of an enemy; unfriendly

9   **a** _ _ _   a male child
    b _ _ _ _ _ _ _   to refuse to have anything to do with

10   **a** _ _ _ _   a lump; a large quantity together
     b _ _ _ _ _ _ _ _   wholesale; pitiless slaughter

B

In a certain code the figures stand for the word

5	2	9	7	4	6	3	1	8
C	O	M	P	A	N	I	E	S

Write the words for:

1 **8 5 4 9 7**
2 **5 2 9 1 8**
3 **7 4 6 3 5**
4 **8 6 3 7 1**
5 **8 7 4 5 1**

Write the figures for:

6   C A P E S
7   O P E N S
8   S P I C E
9   P I A N O
10   S C O N E

Using the right adjective

A   Copy the adjectives in column **a** in your exercise book in the order given. Opposite each write the noun in column **b** which matches it.

a	b
frantic	slope
antique	allowance
affectionate	drugs
formidable	grip
palatable	clothes
injurious	daughter
threadbare	struggles
meagre	task
precipitous	furniture
relentless	meal

B   Choose the word from the list on the left which will complete each sentence correctly.

shrewd
vivid
candid
riotous
abundant
luscious
secluded
righteous
sumptuous
prosperous

1   The traveller had many _____ memories of his jungle adventures.

2   The peach is a _____ fruit.

3   Sir Walter is the managing director of a _____ business.

4   The _____ businessman made a profit.

5   A _____ feast was held in the emperor's honour.

6   The boys were rocking with _____ laughter.

7   The town is proud of its _____ supply of water.

8   He gave them his _____ opinion of their actions.

9   At the bottom of the garden was a _____ nook with an oak seat beneath a shady tree.

10   The insult filled the woman with _____ indignation.

Pronouns

a John told Susan that John would lend Susan a book.

b John told Susan that **he** would lend **her** a book.

Instead of repeating the word **John**, the word **he** is used in (**b**).

Instead of repeating the word **Susan**, the word **her** is used.

A word which is used instead of a noun is called a pronoun.

```
herself

her
it                    itself
```

A Rewrite these sentences, using pronouns from the list on the left in place of the words in bold type.

he
it
we
us
she
her
his
him
them
they

1 Anne told Jennifer that **Anne** would knit a cardigan for **Jennifer**.

2 When Colin was given a dog **Colin** trained **the dog** to beg.

3 Brian and I are good friends. **Brian and I** go everywhere together.

4 As Roger and I approached the farmyard gate a big dog barked at **Roger and me**.

5 The teacher sent for Robin and Alan. The teacher told **Robin and Alan** to stay in after school.

6 The two girls knew that **the two girls** would be late.

7 Andrew was sad because the stolen bicycle was **Andrew's**.

B Insert one of the pronouns in the list on the left in each sentence.

myself
itself
yourself
ourselves
yourselves
herself

1 You boys must make _____ useful in the garden.

2 Did you make this table _____ , Spencer?

3 The hedgehog can roll _____ into a prickly ball.

4 I can work the sum by _____ , thank you.

5 Janet certainly thinks _____ somebody of importance.

6 We built the house _____ .

Homophones

Some words are pronounced like other words but are different in spelling and meaning,
e.g. main, mane
     bear, bare.

Such words are called homophones.

air	what we breathe
heir	one entitled to a dead person's property
allowed	permitted
aloud	loud enough to be heard
beach	the sea-shore
beech	a tree
boy	a male child
buoy	a floating marker for ships
brake	a device to check speed
break	to cause something to come into pieces
cereal	wheat, barley and oats are all cereals
serial	a story or film appearing in parts
check	to stop; a squared pattern
cheque	an order to a bank to pay money
coarse	rough
course	a track; an onward movement
currant	a dried grape
current	a flow of water, air, etc.
foul	filthy; wicked; vile
fowl	a bird

A   Choose the correct word from the pair above to complete each sentence.

1   **cereal   serial**
Cornflakes are his favourite _____.

2   **currant   current**
These _____ buns are delicious.

3   **foul   fowl**
Fulham were awarded a free-kick for a _____ on their goalkeeper.

4   **air   heir**
Prince Charles is _____ to the throne.

5   **break   brake**
New blocks had to be fitted to the front _____ of the bicycle.

B   Write five pairs of words to complete these sentences.

1   Father paid by _____ for his new _____ suit.

2   The _____ who fell overboard swam to a nearby _____ .

3   Talking _____ is not _____ in the reading room of the library.

4   Racing was difficult because the grass on the _____ was long and _____ .

5   Not far from the sandy _____ grew a clump of _____ trees.

Abbreviations

Abbreviations are shortened forms of words or phrases.

Learn this list, then do the exercises.

A.A.	Automobile Association
c/o	care of
Dept.	Department
H.R.H.	His (Her) Royal Highness
J.P.	Justice of the Peace
Ltd.	Limited
M.D.	Doctor of Medicine
M.P.	Member of Parliament
M.O.H.	Medical Officer of Health
N.S.P.C.C.	National Society for the Prevention of Cruelty to Children
O.H.M.S.	On Her Majesty's Service
p.c.	postcard
R.N.	Royal Navy
R.S.P.C.A.	Royal Society for the Prevention of Cruelty to Animals
U.N.	United Nations
Tel.	Telephone; Telegraph

A . Write the meanings of the abbreviations in bold type.

1 The widow wrote to her **M.P.** about her compensation.

2 The letter was addressed to the Sales **Dept**.

3 An inspector of the **N.S.P.C.C.** called to inspect the house.

4 Tim's holiday address is **c/o** Mrs. Baines, 15 High St., Burland.

5 A large crowd gathered to greet **H.R.H.** Princess Margaret.

6 The matter has been reported to the **R.S.P.C.A.**

7 I will send you a **p.c.** as soon as I arrive.

8 The warrant for the arrest of the culprit was signed by a **J.P.**

B Give the meaning of each abbreviation in bold type.

1 On the notepaper was printed: **Tel.** Bury 2385.

2 No postage is payable on letters and parcels sent **O.H.M.S.**

3 The building of the **R.N.** Barracks at Devonport was begun in 1879.

4 The **A.A.** was founded in London in 1905.

5 Both Britain and America are members of the **U.N.**

6 A lecture on the evils of smoking was given by Charles Rennie, **M.D.**

7 The **M.O.H.** told people to boil all drinking water.

Rikki-tikki and Darzee

Then Rikki-tikki went out into the garden to see what was to be seen. It was a large garden, only half-cultivated, with bushes as big as summer-houses of Marshal Niel roses, lime and orange trees, clumps of bamboo, and thickets of high grass. Rikki-tikki licked his lips. "This is a splendid hunting-ground," he said, and his tail grew bottle-brushy at the thought of it, and he scuttled up and down the garden, snuffing here and there till he heard very sorrowful voices in a thornbush.

It was Darzee, the tailor-bird, and his wife. They had made a beautiful nest by pulling two big leaves together and stitching them up the edges with fibres, and had filled the hollow with cotton and downy fluff. The nest swayed to and fro, as they sat on the rim and cried.

"What is the matter?" asked Rikki-tikki.

"We are very miserable," said Darzee. "One of our babies fell out of the nest yesterday, and Nag ate him."

"H'm!" said Rikki-tikki, "that is very sad – but I am a stranger here. Who is Nag?"

Darzee and his wife only cowered down in the nest without answering, for from the thick grass at the foot of the bush there came a low hiss – a horrid cold sound that made Rikki-tikki jump back two clear feet. Then inch by inch out of the grass rose up the head and spread hood of Nag, the big black cobra, and he was five feet long from tongue to tail.

The Jungle Book   Rudyard Kipling.

1 Why did Rikki-tikki lick his lips?
2 What change came over Rikki-tikki's tail as he thought about this?
3 What did Rikki-tikki hear as he scuttled up and down the garden?
4 How do tailor-birds make a nest?
5 Why were Darzee and his wife crying?
6 Where did the low hiss come from?
7 What did Darzee and his wife do when they heard this noise?
8 What effect did this sound have on Rikki-tikki?
9 How long was Nag from tongue to tail?

Letter writing

Alastair Brooks saw this advertisement in a magazine.

FREE

The REX packet of 100 different foreign stamps to applicants for our approval sheets and illustrated catalogue.
Enclose stamp for postage.
Rex Stamp Co. Ltd., 146 Forsyth Rd., London NW5 2BQ

Rex Stamp Co. Ltd.,
146 Forsyth Road,
London NW5 2BQ

19 Jubilee Road,
Granton,
Kent GN74CP

Rex Stamp Co. Ltd.,
146 Forsyth Road,
London NW5

Dear Sirs,

Please send me the Rex free packet of foreign stamps, also a selection of approval sheets and a copy of your illustrated catalogue.

I enclose stamps for postage.

Yours faithfully,
Alastair Brooks.

This is how he addressed the envelope.

This is the letter he wrote.

Points to remember:

a Keep to the form of letter shown, giving your full address.

b State exactly what you require, making your letter as brief as possible.

c If requested to enclose stamps or a postal order, make sure you do so.

d Address the envelope plainly and fully, and see that it bears a stamp for the correct postage.

1 Write a letter to the Planet Novelty Co. Ltd., 49 Greenham Avenue, London E12 SA16 for a copy of their price-list of conjuring tricks, enclosing stamps for postage.

2 The Medico Co. Ltd., Grove Buildings, Anson Street, Birmingham B12 4EH, offer a free sample tube of Atlas toothpaste to all applicants enclosing stamps for postage. Send for a sample.

3 Write to the Mekko Model Co. Ltd., 37 Bilton Road, London SE16 8RL for a copy of their illustrated catalogue of model railways, aircraft, racing cars and boats, which will be sent post free.

Occupations

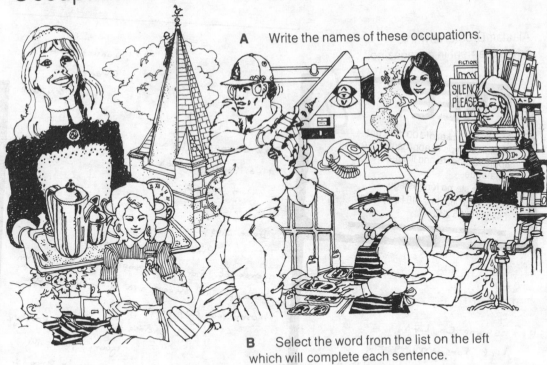

A   Write the names of these occupations.

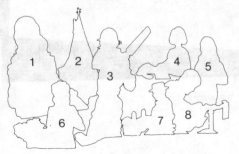

announcer   plumber
postwoman   butcher
chef   chemist
florist   waitress
nurse   steeplejack
jeweller   tobacconist
librarian   undertaker
cricketer   upholsterer

B   Select the word from the list on the left which will complete each sentence.

1   The ____ at the public library has three excellent assistants.

2   The ____ at the corner sells lots of different sweets and chocolates.

3   The ____ at the beach café served us with tea very quickly.

4   The ____ had a large selection of medicines and pills.

5   The ____ offered Maisie a gold watch at a reduced price.

6   The twins went to the ____ to buy their mother a bouquet of flowers.

7   The ____ displays all his meats on trays in his shop window.

8   The ____ climbed to the top of the church steeple to inspect the damage done by the gale.

9   Our ____ uses her bicycle on her rounds.

10 The ____ took Tom's temperature and pulse every four hours.

Group names

A Give the name of the group to which these objects belong.

B Choose the word in the column on the left which belongs to each of the groups below. Give the name of each group.

Example 1 **venison** names of meats

baker
silver
alligator
synagogue
villa
venison

1	beef	2 cathedral	3 cobra
	pork	temple	crocodile
	lamb	church	adder
	mutton	chapel	lizard
4	house	5 copper	6 grocer
	bungalow	gold	butcher
	mansion	iron	fruiterer
	cottage	lead	fishmonger

C Draw four columns and write the headings:

Weapons   Vessels   Furniture   Footwear

Then place the words below in their correct groups. There will be six words in each group.

liner	sandals	spear	wardrobe
clogs	submarine	boots	pistol
cupboard	dagger	sideboard	cruiser
rifle	armchair	yacht	cabinet
trawler	shoes	sword	wellingtons
table	schooner	slippers	revolver

Comparing adjectives

There are **three** degrees of adjectives.

1 The **positive degree**.
Used for one person or thing e.g. tall

2 The **comparative degree**.
Used in comparing two persons or things e.g. taller

3 The **superlative degree**.
Used in comparing more than two persons or things e.g. tallest

We can add **-er** and **-est** to many adjectives without any change in spelling, e.g. strong, stronger, strongest.

But look out for these spelling changes.

a Dropping final **e**.
e.g. wide, wider, widest

b Changing **y** to **i**.
e.g. happy, happier, happiest

c Doubling the last letter.
e.g. hot, hotter, hottest.

When comparing longer adjectives the words **more** and **most**, or **less** and **least** are placed before them.

Example
Jill is the **most reliable** person for the job.

Roger is **fat**.   Rex is **fatter**.

A   Copy and complete this table.

Positive degree	Comparative degree	Superlative degree
1 lovely	_____	_____
2 large	_____	_____
3 hot	_____	_____
4 noisy	_____	_____
5 slim	_____	_____
6 wise	_____	_____
7 wet	_____	_____
8 wealthy	_____	_____
9 fine	_____	_____
10 greedy	_____	_____

B   Complete each sentence, using the **comparative degree** or the **superlative degree** of the adjective in bold type.

1 Robinson is the _____ workman of the two.   **capable**

2 She is easily the _____ girl of the whole school.   **intelligent**

3 Julian is the _____ of the two brothers.   **generous**

Angus is the **fattest**.

4 Jean chose the _____ dress in the shop. **expensive**

5 A miner's work is _____ than a farmer's. **dangerous**

6 Many people consider the Taj Mahal to be the _____ building in the world. **wonderful**

7 The manager has the _____ job in the works. **important**

8 This is the _____ book of the two. **interesting**

Some adjectives cannot be compared in the ways shown; they are irregular.

Positive degree	Comparative degree	Superlative degree
good	better	best
bad	worse	worst
ill	worse	worst
many	more	most
much	more	most
little	less	least

C Write the correct degree of the adjective which will complete each sentence.

1 This is the _____ blizzard I have ever seen. **bad**

2 The patient was very ill yesterday but he is even _____ today. **ill**

3 Both boys read well, but David is the _____ reader. **good**

4 Your cold is _____ than mine. **bad**

5 Dorothy is the _____ singer in the school choir. **good**

6 August is the month when guest-houses have the _____ bookings. **many**

7 £1 is the _____ amount that can be invested. **small**

8 Geoffrey has little common sense; Francis has even _____ . **little**

29

The score card

Below you will find the first innings score card of the Kenville Cricket Club in their annual match against Royford Cricket Club. Look at the questions which follow, study the score card, and then write your answers.

Kenville – First innings

R. Dale; b Gibson	41
J. W. Gray; c Jagger, b Barlow	52
B. R. Lock; lbw Rank	27
W. Smith; c Jagger, b Rank	9
A. Booth; c Robinson, b Moss	83
T. E. Dexter; not out	35
C. Green; c and b Gibson	6
E. F. Clark; st Jagger, b Moss	1
L. Jones; c Thomson, b Moss	0
D. Macmillan; b Moss	0
S. Taylor; st Jagger, b Rank	3
Extras	8
Total	

1 Who was the highest scorer?

2 How many short of a century was his score?

3 How many batsmen were clean bowled? Who were they?

4 Who was bowled for a "duck"?

5 Which bowler made a catch off his own bowling?

6 Which of the batsmen was undefeated at the end of the innings?

7 Who was caught before he had scored?

8 Who was out leg before wicket?

9 What was the name of Royford's wicket-keeper?

10 Do you think he played well or not? Give reasons for your answer.

11 One of the four bowlers performed the "hat trick". Who do you think this was?

12 How many runs will Royford have to make for a first innings lead?

Conjunctions

Paul closed his book.
He put it away.   *two sentences*

Paul closed his book **and** put
it away.   *one sentence*

The word **and** joins the two
sentences.

**A word which joins two groups
of words or two sentences
is called a conjunction.**

so
as
but
for
and
since
while
because

if
or
after
until
where
unless
although
whether

A   Join each pair of sentences below, using a
suitable conjunction from the list on the left.

1   The boy got out of bed.
    He stretched his arms.

2   We intended to swim.
    The weather was too cold.

3   The cinema was full.
    We went back home.

4   The children made their way home.
    It was getting dark.

5   Ben made some tea.
    His mother bathed the baby.

6   The wind was icy cold.
    It was still winter.

7   She was very unpopular.
    She was so sarcastic.

8   You can do it yourself.
    You are so clever.

B   Insert a suitable conjunction in each space.

1   Would you like a cup of tea ____ would you prefer
    coffee?

2   There will be more accidents at the crossroads
    ____ a roundabout is built there soon.

3   The plan was abandoned ____ much money had
    been spent on it.

4   I enjoyed the film ____ I had seen it before.

5   We intend to go ____ it rains or not.

6   Your arithmetic will improve ____ you always check
    your working.

7   Please do nothing ____ you hear from me.

8   The pupils visited St. Paul's Cathedral ____ they
    were shown the Whispering Gallery.

Opposites using a prefix

The opposites of some words can be formed by writing before them **un**, **in**, **il**, **dis**, **ir** or **im**.

un
aware
certain
favourable
fortunate
grateful
important
kind
necessary
popular
usual

in
considerate
efficient
equality
frequent
gratitude
human
sane

il
legal

dis
appear
approve
connect
continue
courteous
honest
obedient
orderly
regard
similar

ir
regular
responsible
reverent

im
movable
patient
perfect
probable
proper

A   Form the opposites of these words, using prefixes.

1 sane
2 aware
3 human
4 usual
5 obedient
6 approve
7 equality
8 similar
9 certain
10 perfect
11 gratitude
12 regard
13 continue
14 considerate
15 orderly

B   Select a word from the list to complete each sentence.

1 An ____ event is one which will probably never happen.

2 An object which cannot be moved is ____ .

3 An ____ person gives no thanks for kindnesses received.

4 Another word for ____ is unlawful.

5 An ____ person is not responsible for his actions.

6 An ____ article is one you can do without.

7 The word ____ means unlucky.

8 A ____ person is rude and ill-mannered.

C   Use these phrases in sentences of your own, but give the word in bold type an opposite meaning.

1 a **popular** man
2 **regular** attendance
3 an **efficient** worker
4 an **important** town
5 **favourable** weather
6 a **proper** remark

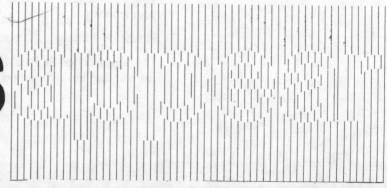

32

People

exile	A person banished from his native country
genius	An exceptionally brainy or gifted person
hypocrite	Pretends to be better than he really is
lunatic	A person who is mad
mimic	Imitates the voice and actions of others
pedestrian	Travels about on foot
prophet	Foretells coming events
traitor	Betrays his country, friends or any trust
tyrant	Uses his power to oppress others
vandal	Wilfully damages or destroys property

PEDESTRIANS ONLY

A Give one word for each of the following.

1 A person who attends church regularly yet leads an evil life in secret

2 A man who sells his country's secrets to a foreign power

3 A king who treats his subjects harshly

4 A person who is not in his right mind

5 A person who has not seen his native land for many years

B Complete each sentence by using a word from the list.

1 The event was foretold by a ____ who lived in Israel.

2 A ____ who crossed the road without looking both ways was knocked down by a car.

3 Shakespeare, who wrote some of the world's best plays, was a ____ .

4 A ____ had uprooted shrubs in the park and smashed several windows in the pavilion.

5 The ____ in the variety show gave wonderful imitations of television stars.

Proper adjectives

A **proper adjective** is one formed from a **proper noun**, which is the name of a particular person, place or thing.

Alps	Alpine
Belgium	Belgian
China	Chinese
Cyprus	Cypriot
Denmark	Danish
Finland	Finnish
Greece	Greek
Holland	Dutch
Iceland	Icelandic
Israel	Israeli
Malta	Maltese
Mexico	Mexican
Norway	Norwegian
Poland	Polish
Portugal	Portuguese
Spain	Spanish
Sweden	Swedish
Switzerland	Swiss
Turkey	Turkish
Venice	Venetian

A Copy these phrases, inserting in each the **proper adjective** formed from the proper noun in bold type.

1 A ____ dance **Spain**
2 A ____ goddess **Greece**
3 ____ bacon **Denmark**
4 A ____ restaurant **China**
5 ____ bulbs **Holland**
6 ____ oranges **Israel**
7 A ____ cross **Malta**
8 The ____ fiords **Norway**
9 An ____ village **Alps**
10 ____ timber **Sweden**

B Complete each sentence below by using a **proper adjective** from the list on the left.

1 Many Britons spend their holidays on the ____ coast. **Belgium**

2 Tampico is a ____ port. **Mexico**

3 Many ____ refugees have settled down in Britain. **Poland**

4 ____ watches are renowned for their reliability. **Switzerland**

5 A fez is a felt cap with a long tassel formerly worn by ____ men. **Turkey**

6 ____ wines are famous, the best known being Port Wine. **Portugal**

7 Thousands of fish were landed by the ____ trawlers. **Iceland**

8 The long narrow boats used on ____ canals are called gondolas. **Venice**

Nouns possession

To make a **singular** noun show possession add **'s**.

Examples

the apron belonging to mother
mother**'s** apron

the beak of the duck
the duck**'s** beak

To make a **plural** noun **ending with s** show possession add **'**.

Examples

the football belonging to the boys
the boys**'** football

the necks of the swans
the swans**'** necks

To make a **plural** noun **which does not end with s** show possession, add **'s** just as with a singular noun.

Examples

the work of the men
the men**'s** work

fashions for women
women**'s** fashions

A

1   the dress belonging to Ann
2   the sword belonging to the knight
3   the thimble belonging to the tailor
4   the block belonging to the butcher
5   the pads belonging to the cricketer
6   the jaws of the lion
7   the reward of the winner
8   the gloves of the boxer
9   the jokes of the comedian

B

1   the lamps belonging to the miners
2   the tusks belonging to the elephants
3   the quarters belonging to the sailors
4   the room belonging to the porters
5   the playground belonging to the girls
6   the tails of the monkeys
7   the wings of the insects
8   the nests of the birds
9   the cloakroom for ladies

C

1   handbags for women
2   the yokes belonging to the oxen
3   the tails belonging to the mice
4   the helmets belonging to the policemen
5   toys for children
6   shoes for men
7   the camp of the airmen
8   the feet of the frogmen
9   the honks of the geese

Sea-lions

Sea-lions bear some resemblance to seals, though they are much larger. When fully grown they are from twelve to twenty feet in length, and from eight to fifteen feet in circumference; they are extremely fat, so that having cut through the skin, which is about an inch in thickness, there is at least a foot of fat before you come to either lean or bones.

Their skins are covered with short grey hair, but their tails and their fins, which serve them for feet on shore, are almost black. They have a distant resemblance to an overgrown seal, though in some particulars there is a manifest difference between them, especially in the males. These have a large snout, or trunk, hanging down five or six inches below the end of the upper jaw, which the females have not.

These animals divide their time equally between the land and the sea, continuing at sea all the summer, and coming on shore at the setting in of winter, where they reside during the whole of that season. In this interval they bring forth their young, and have generally two at a birth, which they suckle with their milk, they being at first about the size of a full-grown seal. During the time these sea-lions continue on shore, they feed on the grass and small plants which grow near the banks of fresh-water streams.

They often, especially the males, have furious battles with each other, principally about their females; and we were one day surprised by the sight of two sea-lions goring each other with their teeth until they were covered with blood.

Anson's Voyage Round the World   Richard Walter

1   Which is the bigger, a sea-lion or a seal?
2   What is the length of a fully grown sea-lion?
3   What is the thickness of a sea-lion's skin?
4   What thickness of fat lies between the skin of a
     sea-lion and its flesh or bones?
5   What purpose is served by the sea-lion's tail and fins
     when it is on shore?
6   Where does the sea-lion spend the summer?
7   Where does it spend the winter?
8   At what time of year are young sea-lions born?
9   How does the face of a male sea-lion differ from that
     of a female?
10 What do the male sea-lions fight about, chiefly?

Contractions

Can't is a short way of writing **cannot**.

I'll is a short way of writing **I will**

These shortened forms are called **contractions**. Now see how the word **would** is used in contractions.

I would	I'd
she would	she'd
you would	you'd
we would	we'd
he would	he'd
they would	they'd

you would

you **would**

I will

you'd

A   In each sentence write a contraction in place of the words in bold type.

1 The police said **they would** be glad of the information.

2 Our teacher asked us if **we would** like to have a concert.

3 I think **you would** be interested in this book.

4 Father said **he would** give me a football next week.

5 Mother promised **she would** help me to swim.

6 The doctor told me **I would** be better in a few days.

B   Write the contractions for the following.

1	I am	11	have not
2	you have	12	she will
3	she is	13	I would
4	will not	14	we are
5	he would	15	are not
6	do not	16	you are
7	they are	17	we would
8	shall not	18	they have
9	we have	19	cannot
10	it is	20	they will

C   Write the words for which the contractions stand.

1 I **can't** forget that **I'm** bereft
Of all the pleasant sights they see.
The Pied Piper of Hamelin

2 Said Francis then, "Faith, gentlemen, **we're** better here than there."
The Glove and the Lions

3 The old sage said, "**You're** as sound as a nut."
The Enchanted Shirt

4 Out spoke a wife: "**We've** beds at home;
We'll burn them for a light?"
The Wives of Brixham

Antonyms opposites

absent	present
admit	deny
advance	retreat
arrival	departure
bold	timid
cheap	expensive
conceal	reveal
danger	safety
failure	success
false	true
hollow	solid
hurry	loiter
ignorance	knowledge
innocent	guilty
joy	sorrow
miser	spendthrift
permit	forbid
plentiful	scarce
poverty	wealth
proud	humble

A Write the **opposites** of the following words.

1	joy	7	guilty	13	false
2	miser	8	advance	14	plentiful
3	cheap	9	hollow	15	failure
4	admit	10	arrival	16	poverty
4	permit	11	bold	17	hurry
6	ignorance	12	proud	18	conceal

B Complete each sentence by inserting the **opposite** of the word in bold type.

1 Mother's new coat was quite **cheap**, but her shoes were very ____ .

2 Nine members were **present** and three were ____ .

3 Some of the defendant's statements were **true**, but many were ____ .

4 The old man was a **miser** but his son turned out to be a ____ .

5 Sally always **hurries** home from school but Carol often ____ on the way.

6 ____ is the curse of God; **knowledge** the wing wherewith we fly to heaven. *Shakespeare*

C In each column find the **two antonyms** or opposites.

1	curious	2	plentiful	3	attack
	violent		superior		forbid
	guilty		scarce		receive
	innocent		brilliant		permit

4	timid	5	happiness
	simple		poverty
	huge		thrift
	bold		wealth

reveal

conceal

Direct and indirect speech

Direct speech

''Have you cleaned your teeth, Nigel?'' asked his mother.

The sentence contains the **exact words** spoken by Nigel's mother.

Direct speech always requires inverted commas, or speech marks, '' ' ''.

Indirect speech

Nigel's mother asked him if he had cleaned his teeth.

This sentence does not contain the exact words spoken by Nigel's mother.

Indirect speech does not require inverted commas.

A   Change to **indirect speech**.

1   ''May I have another plum, please Mother?'' asked Philip.

2   ''I have a bad headache, so I think I will lie down,'' said Mr. Dean.

3   ''The days are certainly getting longer,'' remarked Mr. Caldwell.

4   ''Do you know how to play darts, Roger?'' asked David.

5   ''You look as if you could do with a good holiday,'' said Mrs. Smith to her son.

6   ''Peter, wash your hands well before coming to the table,'' said his father.

7   ''Come inside, Mrs. Dale,'' invited the old lady, ''and have tea with us.''

B   Change to **direct speech**

1   The shoe repairer told Robert that his shoes would be ready by Saturday.

2   Simon's mother asked him if he had loitered on the way home from school.

3   Bernard's teacher asked him if he had ever spent a holiday in France.

4   Bernard replied that he had once spent a month in a villa on the Riviera.

5   The headmaster told the boys that their work was improving.

6   Judith told her father that she had come top in English.

7   Her father exclaimed that he was delighted to see her getting on so well and gave her forty pence.

Compound words

A **compound word** is made up of two or more words.

sign + post = signpost

Examples
bookstall toothbrush
matchbox scarecrow

A   Write the names of the objects in the picture below , showing the two words from which each has been formed.

B   In each of these exercises copy the words in column **a** in the order shown, then add a word from column **b** to form a compound word.

	a	b		a	b
1	wood	pocket	1	saw	wreck
2	post	bare	2	waist	wind
3	pen	snake	3	pass	screen
4	sky	cup	4	speed	piece
5	pick	comb	5	fox	wheel
6	break	knife	6	wind	coat
7	honey	pecker	7	ship	glove
8	rattle	water	8	mantel	dust
9	butter	scraper	9	mill	boat
10	thread	box	10	whirl	port

C   In each line join the two words in bold type, beginning with the second word in each case.

1 a **hole** in a garment through which a **button** goes

2 the **worm** which makes **silk**

3 a **hill** thrown up by a **mole**

4 a sheet of **paper** to which **sand** has been glued

5 the **lights** at the **foot** of a stage

Diminutives

A diminutive is a word representing something small or something young.

Examples

kitten
a young cat

booklet
a small book

bear	cub
cod	codling
deer	fawn
dog	puppy
eagle	eaglet
eel	elver
elephant	calf
frog	tadpole
goose	gosling
hare	leveret
horse	foal
mare	filly
owl	owlet
pig	piglet
river	rivulet
sheep	lamb
stream	streamlet
swan	cygnet
whale	calf

A   Write one word for each of the following:

1	a young eel	10	a young cod
2	a baby goose	11	a baby frog
3	a young elephant	12	a young deer
4	a young sheep	13	a young whale
5	a young hare	14	a small river
6	a small stream	15	a young mare
7	a baby owl	16	a young bear
8	a young horse	17	a baby eagle
9	a young dog	18	a young swan

B   Write the words which are missing from these sentences.

1   Several tiny ____ followed the eel up the river.

2   The mare and her ____ trotted round the paddock.

3   The ____ and her leverets lay down in the long grass.

4   The ____ and the foal were sold for £900.

5   The ____ and her lamb grazed in the field.

6   The farmer brought the swill for the sow and her six ____ .

7   A swan and her two ____ floated majestically downstream.

8   The cat carried her ____ in her mouth.

41

The Royal Mint

Hundreds of years ago coins were made in various towns in Britain, including Bristol, Canterbury, London, Winchester and York. After 1810 there was only one Royal Mint, that on Tower Hill, London, but in 1968 a new mint was established at Llantrisant, South Wales, for the manufacture of Britain's decimal currency which was introduced on 15th February 1971.

The metal ingots from which coins are made are melted in closed crucibles for about two hours, and the molten metal is then run into moulds to form coinage-bars which vary in width and thickness according to the coins that are to be made. These bars or strips are next passed between rollers to ensure that they are of uniform size and then put into machines which punch out the blank discs on which the design is to be stamped. After being examined to see that they are of the correct size and shape, these blank discs are fed into annealing drums which soften the metal in preparation for the stamping process. The design is stamped by powerful presses, both sides being done at the same time, and the finished coins are placed on a moving belt for inspection by overlookers who are trained to detect any faults. The newly-minted coins are tested for weight and, after being counted by an automatic machine, are placed in bags, sealed and stored in large strongrooms until required by the banks.

There are no silver coins in Britain's decimal currency, cupro-nickel being used for the 50p, 10p, and 5p pieces.

A sealed bag of 50p pieces contains £250 worth, or 500 coins. Each bag of 10p pieces and 5p pieces contains £100 worth.

1 Name three towns at which coins were made hundreds of years ago.
2 After 1810 there was only one Royal Mint. Where was that?
3 Where was a new Royal Mint established in 1968?
4 When was Britain's decimal currency introduced?
5 How are metal ingots made into coinage-bars?
6 Why are these bars passed between rollers?
7 Why are the blank discs fed into annealing drums?
8 How are the finished coins counted?
9 What metal is used in place of silver for the decimal coins?
10 How many coins would there be in a bag of 5p pieces?

Using the right pronoun

Mistakes are often made in the use of the pronouns **I** and **me**

Which is correct?

Dad and **me** are going to the football match *or*
Dad and **I** are going to the football match.

Make two sentences.

a Dad is going to the football match.
b **I** am going to the football match.

Me am going to the football match would be wrong.

So the correct sentence is

Dad and **I** are going to the football match.

Which is correct?

Uncle George sent a ticket for Dad and **me** *or*
Uncle George sent a ticket for Dad and **I**.

Make two sentences.

a Uncle George sent a ticket for Dad.
b Uncle George sent a ticket for **me**.

Uncle George sent a ticket for **I** would be wrong.

So the correct sentence is

Uncle George sent a ticket for Dad and **me**.

After the word **between** always use the pronoun **me**.

Example
Between you and **I** he can't afford a new car. (*wrong*)
Between you and **me** he can't afford a new car. (*right*)

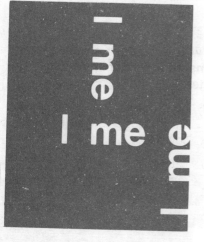

Insert **I** or **me** to complete each sentence.

1 Ann and ____ have won prizes in the drawing competition.

2 Prizes have been awarded to Ann and ____ .

3 June and ____ have been invited to Barbara's party.

4 Barbara has invited June and ____ to her party.

5 This is a secret between you and ____ .

6 You and ____ must keep this matter secret.

7 The headmaster scolded Robert and ____ for being so late.

8 Robert and ____ were scolded by the headmaster for being so late.

9 John and ____ are to share these sweets between us.

10 These sweets are to be shared between John and ____ .

Fun with words

A The second word of each pair is formed from the first word by **changing the first letter**.

1 get let
game lame
goose ____

2 tree free
tour four
table ____

3 bake take
beach teach
brick ____

4 shop chop
slip clip
slash ____

5 crow grow
clean glean
craft ____

B The second word of each pair is formed from the first word by **changing the last letter**.

1 cash cast
fish fist
crush ____

2 mare mark
fore fork
shrine ____

3 read ream
slid slim
hard ____

4 toe ton
ware warn
tore ____

5 car cat
bear beat
boar ____

C The second word of each pair is formed from the first word by **changing one of the inside letters**.

1 bill ball
pine pane
firm ____

2 stay sway
store swore
stitch ____

3 fast fist
mane mine
straps ____

4 meat moat
lead load
beast ____

5 pale pane
mile mine
bold ____

D The second word of each pair is formed from the first word by **inserting a letter immediately after the first letter**.

1 save shave
were where
tread ____

2 bow blow
fat flat
cover ____

3 sack smack
sell smell
site ____

4 sip snip
sore snore
gash ____

5 cat coat
ram roam
vice ____

44

Adjectives formation

Many adjectives are formed by adding **-ous** to a word.

Examples

danger**ous**   prosper**ous**
pomp**ous**   riot**ous**

Sometimes spelling changes are made when **-ous** is added.

1 Drop final **e**.
   famous   porous
   ridiculous   continuous

2 Change **y** to **i**.
   furious   injurious
   envious

3 Double the last letter.
   marvellous   libellous

4 Drop a letter.
   humorous   vigorous
   glamorous

5 Other changes.
   cautious   grievous
   miraculous

Atropa Belladonna

POISONOUS

A   Write the missing **adjectives**. When in difficulty consult your dictionary.

1 A substance which is full of pores is ____ .

2 A person who has won fame is ____ .

3 A person who envies others is ____ .

4 A game which is played with vigour is ____ .

5 A room in which there is plenty of space is ____ .

6 A business which prospers is ____ .

7 Berries which poison are ____ .

8 An adventure in which there is peril is ____ .

9 A person who behaves like a villain is ____ .

10 A person who eats like a glutton is ____ .

B   Complete each sentence by using the **adjective** formed from the word in bold type.

1 The Adventures of Tom Sawyer is a ____ story. **humour**

2 The travellers gazed at the ____ scenery. **marvel**

3 The millionaire lives in a ____ house in France. **luxury**

4 The history of Britain is studded with ____ deeds. **glory**

5 When he heard of the retreat the general was ____ . **fury**

6 Paul has always been a ____ boy. **mischief**

7 Hosepipes were turned on the ____ crowd. **riot**

8 The show is ____ from 5.30 to 11 p.m. **continue**

9 Dense fog and smoke are ____ to health. **injury**

10 The crew of the trawler had a ____ escape from death. **miracle**

Proverbs

Learn these proverbs and their meanings, then answer the questions which follow.

A friend in need is a friend indeed.	Whoever helps you when you are in want is a true friend.
Honesty is the best policy.	To be happy, be honest in all your dealings.
A stitch in time saves nine.	Repairs to any damage now will save bigger repairs later.
A rolling stone gathers no moss.	A person who flits from one job to another will never save money.
Strike while the iron is hot.	Carry out your plans when conditions are favourable.
Necessity is the mother of invention.	When something must be done ways and means of doing it will be found.

A

1 What does a stitch in time do?

2 What is the best policy?

3 What is the mother of invention?

4 What does a rolling stone never gather?

B   Write the proverbs containing the following pairs of words. Some are from Book 3.

1	stone	moss	6	strike	iron
2	coat	cloth	7	stitch	time
3	friend	need	8	necessity	invention
4	feathers	birds	9	birds	flock
5	honesty	policy	10	cooks	broth

C   Complete these proverbs.

1 Strike while the _____ is hot.

2 A friend in _____ is a friend indeed.

3 A _____ in time saves nine.

Similes

When something is very **heavy**
we say it is **as heavy as lead**.

This is because it is similar to
lead in **weight**, although it may
be quite different in other ways.

An expression of this kind is
called a **simile**.

as sweet as sugar
as bold as brass
as brave as a lion
as bright as a button
as busy as a bee
as clean as a new pin
as cool as a cucumber
as dead as a doornail
as deaf as a doorpost
as fit as a fiddle

What are the missing words?

A

1 as bright as a ____
2 as clean as a ____
3 as deaf as a ____
4 as dead as a ____
5 as brave as a ____
6 as ____ as brass
7 as ____ as a fiddle
8 as ____ as a cucumber
9 as ____ as sugar
10 as ____ as a bee

B Book 3

1 as fresh as a ____
2 as cunning as a ____
3 as flat as a ____
4 as proud as a ____
5 as quick as ____
6 as ____ as houses
7 as ____ as a feather
8 as ____ as the hills
9 as ____ as a church mouse
10 as ____ as a rock

C Write the missing words.

1 The old man was as ____ as a doorpost.

2 In walked James as ____ as brass.

3 Old Jacob Marley was as ____ as a doornail.

4 After a hot bath he was as ____ as a new pin.

5 Ann was as busy as a ____ with her knitting.

6 The full-back was as cool as a ____ .

7 Every player in the team was as fit as a ____ .

8 David got up at seven o'clock as bright as a ____ .

47

Inside the vault

James clutched the edge of the stone step. He said to Arnold "Shall I?" and Arnold told him he'd be a silly idiot not to. He got up, rather slowly, and came forward, and lay down on his stomach and shone the torch down into the hole.

It was smaller than he'd expected. A little, crumbling underground room, with rough masonry walls and rubble all over the floor. And long stone boxes stacked up on top of each other: several at one side, one by itself on the other.

Bert's face appeared at the other side of the hole. "Let's have some light over here."

James swung the torch round. They could see the lettering now on top of the solitary box, black-shadowed in the beam of light. "I thought so," said Bert.

> Here lyeth ye body of
> Thomas Kempe Apothecarie
> he departed this life ye last of October AD 1629
> in the 63 yeare of his Age.

"Apothecary?" said James. His voice dropped into the vault, sounding deep and hollow.

"He couldn't go having them put sorcerer, could he?" said Bert. "Not if he wanted to be in here. The Church wouldn't hold with that."

"Why do you think he wanted to be there?" said James in a whisper. "He wasn't very religious, was he? Believing in all that magic, and hating priests."

The Ghost of Thomas Kempe   Penelope Lively

1   Why was the small room very dark?
2   What were the long stone boxes?
3   On which side of the room was Thomas Kempe's box?
4   Give the day and month of Thomas Kempe's death.
5   In what century did Thomas Kempe die?
6   How old was he when he died?
7   What was his occupation as indicated on the box?
8   What was his true occupation?
9   Why could Thomas Kempe not have his true occupation shown on the box?
10 Say in what two ways he was not a religious man.

Joining sentences

On page 31 we learnt how **conjunctions** are used to join two sentences. This can also be done by using **relative pronouns**.

that
which
who
whom
whose

Example
The policeman spoke to the woman.
Her wallet had been stolen.

The policeman spoke to the woman **whose** wallet had been stolen.

It is possible to join together more than two sentences.

Example
Roger likes English.
He likes arithmetic.
He hates history.

Roger likes English **and** arithmetic **but** hates history.

A   Use one of the words from the list on the left to join each pair of sentences.

1   The police arrested the youth.
     He had robbed the bank.

2   Mrs. Baird gave Angela a bracelet.
     It was made of gold.

3   The door was opened by a girl.
     To her I handed the letter.

4   This is the house.
     Jack built it.

5   Sitting near us was a woman.
     Her hair had been dyed blue.

B   Write one sentence in place of each group below.

1   The day was cold.
     The day was windy.
     It was only the first day of February.

2   The dog was barking.
     He was trying to get over the gate.
     The children kept away from him.

3   The office had closed.
     The staff had departed.
     It was not yet five o'clock.

4   I had intended to go for a walk.
     It started to snow.
     I sat by the fire.
     I fell fast asleep.

5   Andrew had a bad leg.
     He was unable to walk.
     He stayed indoors with Gillian.
     She read several stories to him.

6   We set off for the woods.
     After a while there was a thunderstorm.
     We sheltered in an old barn.
     It was close at hand.

Abbreviations

Learn the meaning of each of these abbreviations, then answer the questions which follow.

B.S.T.	British Summer Time
C.I.D.	Criminal Investigation Department
e.g.	for example
G.M.T.	Greenwich Mean Time
i.e.	that is
IOU	I owe you
k.o.	knock-out
m.p.g.	miles per gallon
N.B.	Note well
p.a.	per annum (yearly)
Q.C.	Queen's Counsel
R.S.V.P.	Reply if you please
T.B.	Tuberculosis
v.	versus (against)
via	by way of
viz.	namely

A   Write the meaning of each abbreviation in bold type.

1   The ship will sail from Liverpool on July 9th at 14.30 hours **B.S.T.**

2   As he had no money he gave his creditor an **IOU**.

3   The challenger won by a **k.o.** in the ninth round.

4   We travelled from Cardiff to Bristol **via** the Severn Tunnel.

5   Our car will do 40 **m.p.g.** on a long run.

6   His salary is now £8000 **p.a.**

7   Spurs **v.** Dukla was the match of the year.

8   Two officers of the **C.I.D.** arrived at the scene of the crime.

B

1   The ships' clocks were set by **G.M.T.**

2   Prices are drastically reduced, **e.g.** a £300 bed is now priced at £150.

3   At the bottom of the invitation were the letters **R.S.V.P.**

4   He will inherit the money when he is twenty-one, **i.e.** in 1989.

5   **N.B.** All entries must reach this office by May 26th.

6   For years she has suffered from **T.B.**

7   The accused man was defended by Sir Robert John, **Q.C.**

8   There are seven colours in the rainbow, **viz.** red, orange, yellow, green, blue, indigo and violet.

Using the right verb

Learn how these verbs are used,
then answer the questions.

to **accede** to a **request**
to **avert** a **catastrophe**
to **contract** a **disease**
to **contradict** a **statement**
to **denounce** an **impostor**
to **disperse** a **mob**
to **estimate** the **cost**
to **evade capture**
to **exterminate pests**
to **impart knowledge**
to **impose** a **fine**
to **inflict punishment**
to **inherit** a **fortune**
to **interpret** a **foreign language**
to **liberate** a **prisoner**
to **prophesy** the **future**
to **redeem** a **promise**
to **reveal** a **secret**
to **surmount** an **obstacle**
to **trespass** on **another's land**

A Copy and complete these phrases.

1 to _____ a secret
2 to _____ punishment
3 to _____ capture
4 to _____ knowledge
5 to _____ an obstacle
6 to _____ a prisoner
7 to _____ an impostor
8 to _____ the cost
9 to _____ a disease
10 to _____ on another's land
11 to interpret a _____
12 to inherit a _____
13 to disperse a _____
14 to accede to a _____
15 to prophesy the _____
16 to redeem a _____
17 to exterminate _____
18 to avert a _____
19 to contradict a _____
20 to impose a _____

B Write the verb which will complete each
sentence correctly. Use the past tense where
required.

1 On his father's death he will _____ a million pounds.

2 The magistrates _____ a fine of £50 and costs.

3 Mounted police were brought in to _____ the
demonstrators.

4 The girl who _____ smallpox is seriously ill.

5 A teacher should not only possess knowledge; he
should know how to _____ it.

6 There is to be an all-out effort to _____ rabbits on
farms.

7 For nearly a month the escaped convict _____
capture.

8 The cost of building the new school is _____ at
£6,000,000.

Idioms

In Book 3 you learnt ten sayings which are in common use.

Example

to get into hot water   means to get into trouble

Expressions of this kind are called **idioms**.

Idiom	Meaning
to have an axe to grind	to have something to gain by an action
to be a wet blanket	to be a spoilsport
to draw the long bow	to exaggerate
to make a clean breast of it	to confess to some wrong
to take the bull by the horns	to meet difficulties boldly
to be under a cloud	to be under suspicion
to be a dog in a manger	to deny to others what is useless to oneself
to show the white feather	to show cowardice
to bury the hatchet	to settle a quarrel and live in peace
to flog a dead horse	to do work which produces no results

A   Complete these **idioms** and give the meaning of each.

1   to be under a ___   6   to have an axe ___ ___
2   to flog a ___ horse   7   to take the bull ___ ___ ___
3   to be a dog in a ___   8   to be a wet ___
4   to draw the ___ ___   9   to make a clean ___ ___ ___
5   to bury the ___   10   to show the white ___

B   Rewrite these sentences, substituting the **idiom** for the words in bold type.

1   The detective determined to **meet the difficulties boldly**.

2   Harold told his uncle not to be a **spoilsport**.

3   The old rivals will soon **settle their quarrel and live in peace**.

4   The prefect was **under suspicion** at school.

5   The old sailor is very fond of **exaggerating**.

Synonyms similars

abrupt	sudden
accommodation	room
altitude	height
amiable	friendly
brief	short
comprehend	understand
demonstrate	show
diminutive	small
disperse	scatter
eminent	famous
endeavour	try
interior	inside
intoxicated	drunk
invincible	unbeatable
loathe	hate
melancholy	sad
odour	smell
penetrate	pierce
prohibited	forbidden
reluctant	unwilling

A   Write a simpler word in place of each word in bold type.

1   Smoking in the factory is **prohibited**.

2   The **odour** of fried sausages came from the kitchen.

3   I read a **brief** report of the accident.

4   We failed to obtain **accommodation** at the hotel.

5   This year our cricket team has proved **invincible**.

6   He was most **reluctant** to leave home.

7   We will **endeavour** to deliver the goods today.

8   Mounted police were sent to **disperse** the large crowd.

9   The plane was flying at an **altitude** of 10,000 metres.

10   Our train came to an **abrupt** stop.

B   In each group below select the word which is similar in meaning to the word in bold type.

1 **eminent**	2 **intoxicated**	3 **comprehend**
handsome	drunk	fear
skilful	unconscious	understand
famous	sober	pretend

4 **loathe**	5 **demonstrate**	6 **interior**
hate	fight	cheap
adore	squander	inside
respect	show	common

7 **amiable**	8 **melancholy**	9 **penetrate**
rude	sad	thicken
stout	jolly	pierce
friendly	greedy	collapse

10   **diminutive**

tough
dark
small

53

A pony for Jody

Jody could begin to see things now. He looked into the box stall and then stepped back quickly.

A red pony colt was looking at him out of the stall. Its tense ears were forward and a light of disobedience was in its eyes. Its coat was rough and thick as an Airedale's fur and its mane was long and tangled. Jody's throat collapsed in on itself and cut his breath short.

"He needs a good currying," his father said, "and if I ever hear of you not feeding him or leaving his stall dirty I'll sell him off in a minute."

Jody couldn't bear to look at the pony's eyes any more. He gazed down at his hands for a moment, and he asked very shyly: "Mine?" No one answered him. He put his hand out toward the pony. Its grey nose came close, sniffing loudly, and then the lips drew back and the strong teeth closed on Jody's fingers. The pony shook its head up and down and seemed to laugh with amusement. Jody regarded his bruised fingers. "Well," he said with pride – "well, I guess he can bite all right." The two men laughed, somewhat in relief. Carl Tiflin went out of the barn and walked up a side-hill to be by himself, for he was embarrassed, but Billy Buck stayed. It was easier to talk to Billy Buck. Jody asked again – "Mine?"

Billy became professional in tone. "Sure! That is, if you look out for him and break him right. I'll show you how. He's just a colt. You can't ride him for some time."

The Red Pony John Steinbeck

1 Why did Jody step back from the box stall?
2 Which two words indicate the pony's mood and attitude?
3 Why did Jody's throat "collapse in on itself"?
4 What two things did Jody's father warn him he must do?
5 Why couldn't he bear to look at the pony's eye any more?
6 Why did Jody speak of the pony with pride?
7 Why were the two men relieved as they laughed?
8 Why did Carl Tiflin want to be by himself?
9 Why could the pony not be ridden for some time?
10 Who was going to help Jody break in the pony?

Occupations

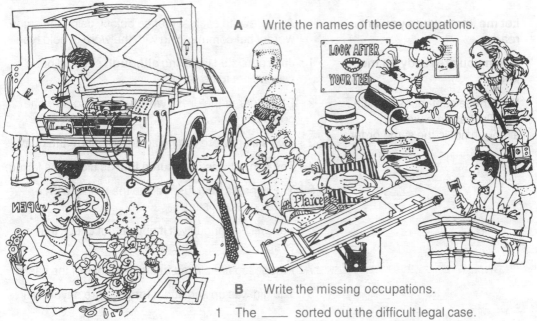

A   Write the names of these occupations.

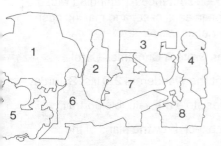

B   Write the missing occupations.

1   The ____ sorted out the difficult legal case.

2   The keen ____ was at the airport to meet the famous actress.

3   The ____ has finished drawing the plans of the school.

4   A ____ and two policemen soon arrived at the scene of the crime.

5   The flowers for the wedding were supplied by the local ____ .

6   I bought some cod and plaice from the ____ .

7   The ____ knocked the piano down at ninety pounds.

8   This is the largest statue the ____ has ever made.

9   The ____ had no difficulty in discovering what was wrong with the car.

architect   fishmonger
auctioneer   florist
author   mechanic
caddie   reporter
chauffeur   sculptor
dentist   solicitor
detective

C   What name is given to a person who:

1   carries a golfer's clubs?
2   sells flowers and plants?
3   writes books and stories?
4   drives his employer's car?
5   examines and repairs teeth?

Sentence structure

Let me know when you are ready.

When you are ready let me know.

Both these sentences contain exactly the same words, although not in the same order.

A   Rewrite each sentence below, using the same words, but commencing with the word in bold type.

1   Julia persisted in talking **although** she had been warned not to do so.

2   She ordered the dress **without** thinking how she could pay for it.

3   Two sailors were having an argument **on** the quay.

4   The convict was recaptured **just** as night was falling.

5   The express train rushed into the tunnel **with** a shriek of its whistle.

6   You will be seriously ill **if** you do not check that cough.

7   A huge log fire blazed **in** the great hall of the castle.

8   The girl was up and about **long** before daybreak.

a   A rattlesnake **bit** the lumberjack.

b   The lumberjack **was bitten** by a rattlesnake.

Both these sentences convey the same idea, but the words they contain are not exactly the same.

(**a**) contains the word **bit**, the Past Tense of bite.

(**b**) contains the word **bitten**, the Past Participle of bite.

B   Rewrite these sentences, beginning with the word in bold type in each case, and making such changes as are necessary.

1   Charles Dickens wrote **A** Christmas Carol.

2   The Rovers beat **the** Wanderers 2-0 last Saturday.

3   A gang of thieves stole **the** valuable portrait.

4   The County Architect drew **the** plans of the dining-hall.

5   The heavy fall shook **the** frail old gentleman.

6   The twins took **Spot** to the park.

7   Our puppy tore **that** curtain.

8   The three girls chose **the** curtains for the lounge.

Alphabetical order

A Arrange the words in each group in alphabetical order. Look at the **fifth** letter of each word.

1	straw	2	handicap	3	catapult
	strap		handy		catastrophe
	straight		handsome		catalogue
	stray		handle		catacomb
	strand		handful		cataract

4	fortress	5	partner	6	compile
	fortunate		partly		complain
	fortify		partake		compel
	forth		party		compose
	fortnight		partial		compare

This is a drawing of a ten-volume encyclopaedia. Each volume is numbered and also shows the first four letters of the first word and the last word it contains.

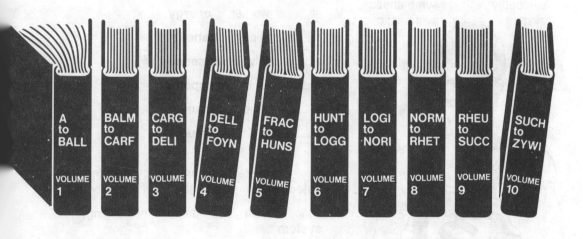

A to BALL	BALM to CARF	CARG to DELI	DELL to FOYN	FRAC to HUNS	HUNT to LOGG	LOGI to NORI	NORM to RHET	RHEU to SUCC	SUCH to ZYWI
VOLUME 1	VOLUME 2	VOLUME 3	VOLUME 4	VOLUME 5	VOLUME 6	VOLUME 7	VOLUME 8	VOLUME 9	VOLUME 10

B Give the numbers of the volumes in which you would look for the following words.

1	longitude	8	athletics	15	foundry
2	Dunlop	9	portcullis	16	decimal
3	meteor	10	Henry VIII	17	resin
4	indigo	11	Kiel Canal	18	Napoleon
5	cardinal	12	gannet	19	shorthand
6	balsa	13	vodka	20	crypt
7	tambourine	14	Jolly Roger		

Adjectives formation

Noun	Adjective
athlete	athletic
benefit	beneficial
circle	circular
credit	creditable
custom	customary
effect	effective
energy	energetic
fire	fiery
fraud	fraudulent
giant	gigantic
influence	influential
metal	metallic
method	methodical
muscle	muscular
nonsense	nonsensical
picture	picturesque
science	scientific
skill	skilful
sympathy	sympathetic
system	systematic

A   Form **adjectives** from these nouns.

1 muscle   7 skill   13 science
2 effect   8 benefit   14 fire
3 fraud   9 system   15 picture
4 athlete   10 credit   16 influence
5 sympathy   11 method   17 circle
6 energy   12 giant   18 metal

B   Write the missing **adjectives**.

1 an ____ remedy   **effect**

2 a ____ craftsman   **skill**

3 a ____ sound   **metal**

4 an ____ man   **athlete**

5 a ____ age   **science**

6 a ____ saw   **circle**

7 an ____ worker   **energy**

8 a ____ holiday   **benefit**

9 a ____ reply   **nonsense**

10 a ____ friend   **sympathy**

11 a ____ scene   **picture**

12 a ____ scheme   **fraud**

C   Complete each sentence by inserting the **adjective** formed from the noun in bold type.

1 Police made a ____ search of the building. **system**

2 The scientist is noted for his ____ work.   **method**

3 Paul's success was a most ____ achievement. **credit**

4 The key was not in its ____ place.   **custom**

5 We stayed at a ____ Cornish fishing village. **picture**

Capital letters

Capital letters are used for:

names of persons
pets
days
months *but not seasons*
special holidays
geographical names
nations
languages
titles of books, poems, songs, etc.

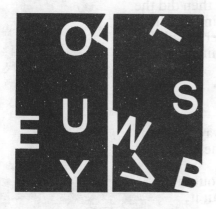

A Rewrite these sentences, using capital letters where necessary.

1 the river thames is sometimes referred to as old father thames.

2 both german and italian are taught at grosvenor grammar school.

3 rudyard kipling, who was born in india, wrote many fine books, the most famous being the jungle books.

4 easter is a movable festival which may come in march or april, but christmas is not.

5 the bank of england is sometimes called the old lady of threadneedle street.

6 linda's brother colin is a patient at the middlesex hospital.

7 the white tower in the tower of london was built by gundulf, bishop of rochester, about A.D. 1078.

8 from monday to friday the shop closes at 5.30; on saturdays it closes at 1 o'clock.

B Copy these sentences and insert punctuation marks in each.

1 Would you like to tour Europe and see its wonderful sights

2 In the market there were ample supplies of apples pears oranges bananas peaches and grapes

3 James did you give my message to the headmaster asked his mother

4 Yes Mother I gave it to him before lessons began replied James

5 Some members wont be present but it doesnt matter

6 The ticket bore the date Thurs 26th Sept in bold type

7 The bat we played with was Toms but the ball was Duncans.

8 Oh dear exclaimed Miss Taylor in alarm I have lost my purse

Encounter with a dinosaur

Something was swimming toward the lighthouse tower.

It was a cold night, as I have said; the high tower was cold, the light coming and going, and the Fog Horn calling and calling through the ravelling mist. You couldn't see far and you couldn't see plain, but there was the deep sea moving on its way about the night earth, flat and quiet, the colour of grey mud, and here were the two of us alone in the high tower, and there, far out at first, was a ripple, followed by a wave, a rising, a bubble, a bit of froth. And then, from the surface of the cold sea came a head, a large head, dark-coloured, with immense eyes, and then a neck. And then – not a body – but more neck and more! The head rose a full forty feet above the water on a slender and beautiful dark neck. Only then did the body, like a little island of black coral and shells and crayfish, drip up from the subterranean. There was a flicker of tail. In all, from head to tail, I estimated the monster at ninety or a hundred feet.

I don't know what I said. I said something.

"Steady, boy, steady," whispered McDunn.

"It's impossible!" I said.

"No, Johnny, *we're* impossible. *It's* like it always was ten million years ago. It hasn't changed. It's *us* and the land that've changed, become impossible. *Us!*"

It swam slowly and with a great dark majesty out in the icy waters, far away. The fog came and went about it, momentarily erasing its shape.

The Fog Horn   Ray Bradbury

1   On what kind of night did this story take place?
2   What sound could be heard?
3   How much visibility was there?
4   Which movement first told the men there was something in the sea?
5   Where did the men first see this movement?
6   At what height above the water did the head rise?
7   To what does the writer compare the monster's body?
8   How long was the monster?
9   When did McDunn suggest these monsters had once lived?
10 Why was the monster not continuously visible?

Homophones

herd	a number of animals together
heard	past tense of hear
key	locks a door, etc.
quay	a landing-place for ships
night	time between evening and morning
knight	a titled gentleman
muscle	part of the body
mussel	a shellfish
place	a particular part of space
plaice	a flat-fish
profit	gain; benefit
prophet	one who foretells events
sew	to work with needle and thread
sow	to scatter seed
stile	steps in a fence or wall
style	fashion
vale	a valley
veil	thin material covering the face
stationery	writing materials
stationary	standing still

A Choose the correct word from the pair above to complete each sentence.

1 **vale   veil**
The bride wore a ____ of lace.

2 **stationery   stationary**
The fast sports car collided with a ____ saloon car.

3 **profit   prophet**
The ____ foretold the defeat of the Hebrews.

4 **sow   sew**
In spring farmers plough their fields and ____ the seed.

5 **muscle   mussel**
Having pulled a ____ in his thigh the centre-half had to leave the field.

B Complete each sentence by using a suitable pair of homophones from your list.

1 The thundering hoofs of the stampeding ____ of buffalo could be ____ from a long way off.

2 The ____ to the sailor's chest was found lying on the ____ .

3 The black ____ rode out one ____ to attack the baron's castle.

4 The athlete vaulted over the ____ in fine ____ .

5 The fishmonger put the huge ____ in a prominent ____ on the marble slab.

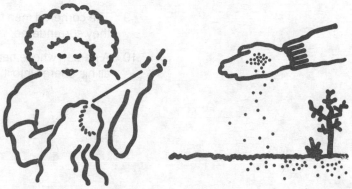

61

Twin words

Many common English expressions consist of two simple words joined by the word **and**.

Learn the expressions in this list. Exercise B shows you how these expressions are used.

flesh and blood
heart and soul
long and short
short and sweet
there and then
thick and thin
tooth and nail
touch and go
ups and downs
ways and means
wear and tear
well and good

A   Copy these expressions and insert the missing words.

1   thick and _____
2   _____ and go
3   there and _____
4   _____ and tear
5   flesh and _____
6   _____ and means
7   long and _____
8   _____ and nail
9   heart and _____
10   _____ and good
11   ups and _____
12   _____ and sweet

B   Write the words needed to complete these sentences.

1   We must consider ways and _____ of building a school swimming bath.

2   The tramp's clothes showed signs of much wear and _____ .

3   The patient recovered from the operation but it was touch and _____ .

4   The discontented film star left the studio _____ and then.

5   The financier had seen many _____ and downs in his life.

6   A loyal friend sticks to you through _____ and thin.

7   The old man had little affection for his own _____ and blood.

8   If you are prepared to accept the responsibility all well and _____

9   The cornered men fought tooth and _____ before they surrendered.

10   A person whose heart and _____ is in his work puts all his energy into it.

Rhymes

farms
be
floors
rye
roars
tower
I
arms
see
devour
doors
sails
me
flails
flour

A Write the words, numbered 1 to 15, which fill the spaces in the verses below.

Behold! a giant am ____   1
Aloft here in my ____ . 2
With my granite jaws I ____   3
The maize, and the wheat and the ____ , 4
And grind them into ____ . 5

I look down over the ____   6
In the fields of grain I ____   7
The harvest that is to ____ , 8
And I fling to the air my ____   9
For I know it is all for ____ . 10

I hear the sound of ____   11
Far off, from the threshing ____ , 12
In barns, with their open ____ , 13
And the wind, the wind in my ____   14
Louder and louder ____ . 15

B Write the word needed to complete each sentence. In each case the missing word rhymes with the word in bold type.

1 He was sorry to have to ____ the invitation. **fine**

2 She will ____ her hundredth birthday tomorrow. **wait**

3 The architect will ____ the site for the school. **play**

4 The rabbit was caught in a ____ . **pair**

5 The ____ against smoking will receive strong support. **main**

6 Wise parents rarely ____ in the quarrels of their children. **deer**

7 When you pay a bill you should obtain a ____ . **meet**

8 ____ furniture is very old and often very valuable. **beak**

9 We are going to ____ our parts for the school play. **purse**

10 The tourists stayed at a ____ village in the Alps. **desk**

63

Prepositions

The dog is **on** the chair.

The dog is **under** the table.

The dog is **in** the car.

The words **in**, **under** and **on** show how the word 'dog' is related to the words **car**, **table** and **chair**.

A word which shows the relationship between a noun (or pronoun) and some other word in a sentence is called a preposition.

after	from
against	off
along	on
around	outside
before	through

A   Insert the prepositions in the list on the left in their correct places in the sentences which follow.

1   Judith is suffering _____ influenza.

2   Crowds of people strolled _____ the promenade.

3   Grandpa was seated _____ a blazing fire.

4   Henry leaned _____ the wall of the gymnasium.

5   The dog ran _____ the cat, but could not catch it.

6   Drake was the first Englishman to sail _____ the world.

7   The circus dog jumped right _____ the hoop.

8   A long queue formed _____ the football ground.

9   Lovely water lilies floated _____ the surface of the pond.

10   A workman fell _____ a ladder and was badly hurt.

Using prepositions correctly

between   Things are shared between two persons.

among   Things are shared among more than two.

in   Shows position in one place.
e.g. The budgie was in its cage.

into   Shows movement from one place to another.
e.g. The budgie hopped from the table into its cage.

differ   The twins differ **from** each other in some ways.
I beg to differ **with** you on that point.

different   This book is quite different **from** the one I read last. (Never use **to** or **than** with different.)

beside	Means by the side of.
	e.g. Simon sits beside me in school.
besides	Means in addition to.
	e.g. Another bicycle was stolen besides John's.
	Note that the same word may be followed by different prepositions.

Examples

a I agree **with** you in everything you say.
I hope you will agree **to** my suggestion.

b The headmaster was angry **with** the children.
He was angry **at** their bad behaviour.

c The soldier died **for** his country.
The soldier died **of** wounds.

d The traveller lives **in** Bournemouth.
He lives **at** 27 Broad Street.

e He would not part **with** a penny.
She hates to part **from** her mother.

B Use a **preposition** to complete each sentence.

1 The children were walking about ____ the classroom.

2 The children went from the playground ____ the classroom.

3 Do you agree ____ this proposal?

4 He will agree ____ everything you say.

5 The prize was divided ____ the two winners.

6 The prize was divided ____ several competitors.

7 Angus now lives ____ Edinburgh.

8 He lives with his aunt ____ 49 Argyll Street.

9 The matron stood ____ the patient's bed.

10 He has a private income ____ his large salary.

C Use these phrases in sentences of your own.

1 walked in
2 walked into
3 walked on
4 walked across

5 walked behind
6 walked under
7 walked through
8 walked round

Tarka fights Deadlock

Between boulders and rocks crusted with shellfish and shaggy with seaweed, past worm-channelled posts that marked the fairway for fishing boats at high water, the pack hunted the otter. Off each post a gull launched itself, cackling angrily as it looked down at the animals. Tarka reached the sea. He walked slowly into the surge of a wavelet, and sank away from the chop of old Harper's jaws, just as Deadlock ran through the pack. Hounds swam beyond the line of waves, while people stood at the sea-lap and watched the huntsman wading to his waist. It was said that the otter was dead-beat, and probably floating stiffly in the shallow water. After a few minutes the huntsman shook his head, and withdrew the horn from his waistcoat. He filled his lungs and stopped his breath and was tightening his lips for the four long notes of the call-off, when a brown head with hard dark eyes, was thrust out of the water a yard from Deadlock. Tarka stared into the hound's face and cried "Ic-yang".

The head sank. Swimming under Deadlock, Tarka bit on to the loose skin of the flews and pulled the hound's head under the water. Deadlock tried to twist round and crush the otter's skull in his jaws, but he struggled vainly. Bubbles blew out of his mouth. Soon he was choking. The hounds did not know what was happening. Deadlock's hindlegs kicked the air weakly. The huntsman waded out and pulled him inshore, but Tarka loosened his bite only when he needed new air in his lungs.

Tarka the Otter Henry Williamson

1 Name three physical features that were part of the shore where the otter was hunted.
2 What made the gulls angry?
3 What were the people standing on the shore doing?
4 What did people think had happened to Tarka?
5 Why did the huntsman shake his head?
6 What did he then prepare to do?
7 What prevented him from performing this action?
8 Why was Deadlock's struggle in vain?
9 What part of Deadlock's body was above the surface of the water?
10 Why did Tarka loosen his bite?

Containers

A **caddy** is a container for **tea**.
A **purse** is a container for **money**.

A   Write the names of the containers shown in the pictures.

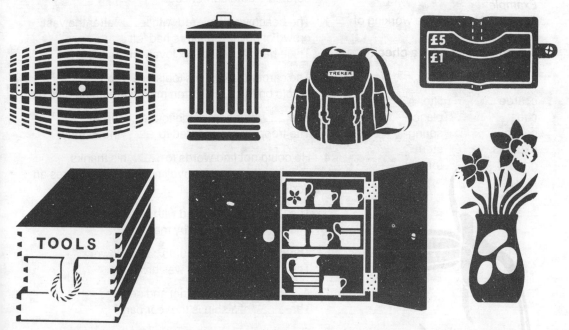

B   Write in order the words which have been omitted from these sentences.

1   The carpenter's tools were kept in a large wooden ____ .

2   The china was packed in straw in a large ____ .

3   Penelope poured the contents of two packets of tea into the ____ .

4   There are piles of plates in the kitchen ____ .

5   Sarah hung her best dress in her mother's ____ .

6   The cowboy put his revolver back in its ____ .

7   The archer took an arrow from his ____ .

8   Many walkers carry a ____ on their backs.

9   The ____ in Black Beauty's stable was piled up with hay.

10   Farmer Giles gave the haymakers a ____ of cider.

barrel	quiver
caddy	rucksack
chest	safe
crate	satchel
cupboard	scabbard
dustbin	scuttle
holster	sheath
kitbag	vase
manger	wallet
purse	wardrobe

Words with more than one meaning

Some words have more than one meaning.

Example
You should **check** the working of every sum.
The bookmaker wore a **check** suit.

charge   litter
chest   plane
coach   spring
express   stern
ground   temple

A   Write the numbers from 1 to 10 in a column, then opposite each write the word which will complete both sentences.

1   The beach was covered with ____ after the vast crowd of holiday-makers had left.
    Trixie had a ____ of six lovely puppies.

2   The carpenter kept his tools in a wooden ____ .
    A cold on the ____ often makes breathing difficult.

3   The ____ for admission to the circus was £1.
    The troops were ordered to ____ the enemy.

4   He could not find words to ____ his thanks.
    The ____ train was travelling at 150 kilometres an hour.

5   The ____ was covered with fallen leaves.
    The coffee was ____ by machinery.

6   The daffodil is my favourite ____ flower.
    The ____ of the clock was broken.

7   A ____ man is very strict and severe.
    The ____ of a ship is the rear part.

8   Carpenters ____ wood to make it smooth.
    The ____ circled the airport twice before landing.

9   Several Hindus were worshipping in the ____ .
    A blow on the ____ rendered the man unconscious.

10 A new master had been appointed to ____ the boys at cricket.
    The motor ____ was carrying thirty-five passengers on a school journey.

B   Use your dictionary to find six words which have more than one meaning. Write sentences to show the different meanings.

Occupations

A Write the names of these occupations.

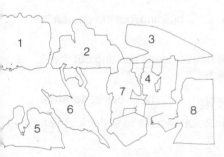

artist   messenger
actress   optician
ballerina   photographer
beautician   physiotherapist
chiropodist   pilot
conjurer   solicitor
engineer   surgeon
interpreter   taxidermist
juggler   teacher
lumberjack   ventriloquist

B Choose the word in your list which will complete each of these sentences correctly.

1 When the ____ had finished stuffing and mounting the barn owl it looked very lifelike.

2 People who travel in foreign countries often need an ____ to make themselves understood.

3 An exhibition of paintings by a local ____ was held in the town hall.

4 She is a trained ____ specializing in skin care.

5 The ____ was forced to make a crash landing.

6 A number of experienced ____ were consulted about the new bridge.

7 The ____ told the magistrates that his client had been assaulted by the defendant.

8 The ____ collected the tickets at the booking office.

9 He has arthritis and is treated by a ____ each week.

10 The ____ performed the heart transplant successfully.

Antonyms opposites

ancient	modern
ascend	descend
attack	defence
captivity	freedom
cautious	reckless
coarse	fine
compulsory	voluntary
defeat	victory
entrance	exit
expand	contract
exterior	interior
famine	glut
import	export
increase	decrease
inferior	superior
majority	minority
maximum	minimum
permanent	temporary
punishment	reward
transparent	opaque

A What are the **opposites** of the following words?

1	expand	10	inferior
2	victory	11	entrance
3	maximum	12	transparent
4	famine	13	cautious
5	coarse	14	descend
6	increase	15	import
7	punishment	16	permanent
8	majority	17	exterior
9	captivity	18	compulsory

B Copy and complete each sentence by inserting the **opposite** of the word in bold type.

1 Both the ___ and the **exit** of the building were well lighted.

2 This file is too ___ ; try a **fine** one.

3 During his long service the general had known both ___ and **defeat**.

4 Service with the Armed Forces was ___ for men and **voluntary** for women.

5 The castle is an ___ building, but the church is quite **modern**.

6 The ___ of the house needs painting but the **interior** is perfect.

7 The team is strong in ___ but weak in **defence**.

8 **Cautious** motorists often have to suffer for the folly of the ___

9 After two years of ___ the prisoners of war thought **freedom** was wonderful.

10 The teacher believed in ___ for the wicked and **reward** for the good.

People

eavesdropper	Listens to conversations not intended for his ears.
emigrant	Leaves his own country to settle in another.
immigrant	Comes into a country and makes his home there.
impostor	Tries to make people think that he is somebody else.
optimist	Always looks on the bright side of life.
pessimist	Looks on the gloomy side of life.
scapegoat	Takes the blame for the misdoings of others.
stowaway	Hides in a ship or plane to avoid paying the fare.
vegetarian	Eats no meat; has fruit, vegetables.
wiseacre	Claims to be very wise.

A Write one word for each of the following.

1 A man who thinks he knows the answer to every question.

2 A person who accepts the blame for a wrong done by another.

3 A person who listens at keyholes.

4 A person who believes that every cloud has a silver lining.

5 A man who goes about posing as a famous general.

B Use one word from the list to complete each sentence.

1 Being a born _____ , Bailey could not help taking a gloomy view of the matter.

2 The _____ was discovered hiding in a hold of the ship.

3 The _____ waved farewell to his relatives as his ship drew away from the quay.

4 Finding meat injurious to his health he decided to become a _____ .

5 The _____ was caught in the act of listening at the keyhole of the manager's door.

Gerard and the bear

Gerard looked wildly down. He was forty feet from the ground. Death below. Death moving slowly but surely upon him in a still more horrible form. The bear crawled on; he saw its open jaws and bloodshot eyes. Hearing a twang he glanced down, and saw Denys shooting up at the bear. The animal snarled at the twang, but crawled on. Again the crossbow twanged, and the next moment the bear was close upon Gerard, who sat on the branch, paralysed. The bear opened her jaws and hot blood spouted from them upon Gerard as from a pump. The bough rocked. The wounded monster was reeling; it stuck its sickles of claws deep into the wood; it toppled, its claws held firm, but its body rolled off, and the sudden shock to the branch shook Gerard forward on his stomach with his face upon one of the bear's straining paws. At this she raised her head up, up, till he felt her hot breath. Then huge teeth snapped together loudly close below him, with a last effort of baffled hate. The ponderous body rent the claws out of the bough, then pounded the earth with a tremendous thump. There was a shout of triumph below, and then a cry of dismay, for Gerard had fainted, and had rolled headlong from the perilous height.

Denys caught at Gerard, and somewhat checked his fall; but it is doubtful whether this alone would have saved him from breaking his neck or a limb. His best friend now was the dying bear, on whose hairy body his head and shoulders safely fell.

The Cloister and the Hearth   Charles Reade

1 How high above the ground was the branch on which Gerard sat?
2 Who was standing beneath this tree?
3 What caused the "twang" which Gerard heard?
4 What did the bear do when she heard this noise?
5 What happened when the bear opened her jaws?
6 Which word tells us that Gerard was unable to move?
7 How was the bear able to cling to the branch although its body had toppled over?
8 What effect did the sudden shock caused by the bear rolling off the branch have upon Gerard?
9 Why was there a cry of dismay from below?
10 Why was the dying bear Gerard's best friend when he fell from the branch of the tree?

Agreement of subject and verb

The **subject** of a sentence must agree with its **verb** in number.

A **singular subject** requires a **singular verb**.

Example
A **cow is** a very useful animal.

A **plural subject** requires a **plural verb**.

Example
Cows are very useful animals.

Now look carefully at this sentence.

A fine **selection** of used cars **was** on view.

The noun **selection**, which is the **subject**, is **singular**, so the singular verb **was** must be used.

Always use a **singular verb** with **each**, **anybody**, **nobody**, **everybody**, **everyone**, **no one**, **either**, **neither**.

Example
Neither of these knives **is** very sharp.

A Choose the correct **verb** from the pair above to complete each sentence.

1 **has   have**
A violet ____ a fragrant smell.

2 **has   have**
Violets ____ a fragrant smell.

3 **wasn't   weren't**
The book ____ on the shelf.

4 **wasn't   weren't**
The books ____ on the shelf.

5 **tries   try**
The boys ____ hard to make good progress.

6 **tries   try**
The boy ____ hard to make good progress.

B Watch for the **subject** in each sentence and use the verb which agrees with it in number.

1 **has   have**
One of the twins ____ very red hair.

2 **has   have**
Both of the twins ____ rosy cheeks.

3 **was   were**
The bunch of keys ____ lost in the street.

4 **was   were**
The keys ____ lost in the street.

5 **makes   make**
A box of chocolates ____ a nice present.

6 **makes   make**
Chocolates ____ a nice present.

7 **is   are**
Road accidents ____ increasing in number.

8 **is   are**
The number of road accidents ____ increasing.

9 **gives   give**
Flowers ____ many people great pleasure.

10 **gives   give**
A bunch of flowers ____ many people pleasure.

Similes

Learn this list of similes, then work the exercises.

as happy as a lark
as mad as a hatter
as meek as a lamb
as patient as Job
as pleased as Punch
as proud as a peacock
as right as rain
as silent as the grave
as slippery as an eel
as smooth as velvet

Complete these similes.

A

1 as right as ____
2 as silent as the ____
3 as pleased as ____
4 as slippery as an ____
5 as happy as a ____
6 as ____ as velvet
7 as ____ as a lamb
8 as ____ as a hatter
9 as ____ as Job
10 as ____ as a peacock

B Revision

1 as cool as a ____
2 as fit as a ____
3 as busy as a ____
4 as deaf as a ____
5 as brave as a ____
6 as ____ as brass
7 as ____ as a new pin
8 as ____ as a doornail
9 as ____ as a button
10 as ____ as sugar

C Write the missing words.

1 Although her children are often naughty, Mrs. Jones is as patient as ____ .

2 Jane's skin is as smooth as ____ .

3 At night most villages are as silent as the ____ .

4 David had to shout loudly because the old man was as deaf as a ____ .

5 The full-back was dazed by the tackle, but after receiving attention from the trainer he was as right as ____ .

6 Martin is as happy as a ____ when playing with his electric railway.

7 Philip was as pleased as ____ with his examination results.

8 The prisoner was as meek as a ____ when he faced the judge.

74

Words which save work

One word can sometimes do the work of several.

Example

People who eat more than is good for them are rarely healthy.

Gluttons are rarely healthy.

accidentally
apologized
author
drought
fearlessly
immediately
librarian
occasionally
postponed
recently
revolved
speechless
surrendered
survivors
talkative

A In each sentence below, replace the words in bold type with a labour-saving word from the list on the left.

1 I met Robert in London **not long ago**.

2 The rebel leader **gave himself up** to the Government forces.

3 Owing to bad weather the school sports had to be **put off to a later date**.

4 Gillian is a bright pupil but rather **fond of talking too much**.

5 After his surprise win Roger was **incapable of speaking**.

6 It is wise to visit the dentist **every now and then**.

7 The **great shortage of rain** has ruined the crops.

8 Of the forty-two passengers in the plane crash, there were only three **who remained alive**.

B

1 The window was broken **by accident**.

2 The hooligans were ordered to leave the cinema **without further delay**.

3 I received a copy of the book of poems from the **man who wrote it**.

4 The policeman tackled the armed robber **without any fear**.

5 Robert asked the **man in charge of the library** if he could recommend the book he had chosen.

6 The chairman of the meeting **expressed his regret** for his late arrival.

7 The blades of the electric fan **turned round and round** at a fantastic speed.

Homophones

bail   **a** money paid to set a person free
      b crosspiece of a wicket

bale   a large bundle

berth   place to sleep on a ship

birth   being born

faint   **a** condition like sleep or death
      b weak; not plain

feint   a sham blow or attack

gilt   thin covering of gold

guilt   state of having done wrong

stake   a pointed stick

steak   a slice of meat or fish

lessen   to grow or make less

lesson   something learnt or taught

root   underground part of a plant

route   a way to go; a road

sight   power or act of seeing

site   position or place

soar   to fly upwards or at a great height

sore   painful

hoard   to save and store up

horde   a crowd, e.g. of hooligans

From the list on the left, choose the correct homophone to complete each sentence.

1 We watched the skylark ____ up into the sky.

2 The champion made a ____ with his left then landed with a punishing right hook.

3 Two of the accused men were released on ____.

4 Our new house is being built on a sunny ____ .

5 On the voyage to America Tony slept on an upper ____ .

6 The prisoner admitted his ____ and was sentenced to three months imprisonment.

7 No sooner had he scored a goal than he was surrounded by a ____ of hooligans.

8 A strong ____ was driven into the earth to support the young apple tree.

9 The tablets he took did much to ____ the pain in his chest.

10 Before we began our tour, Father planned the ____ we were to take.

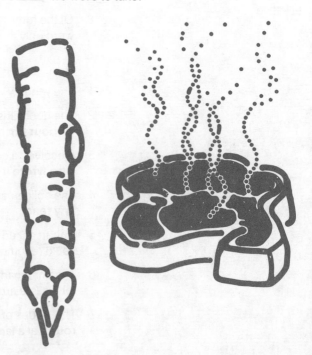

Noises of creatures

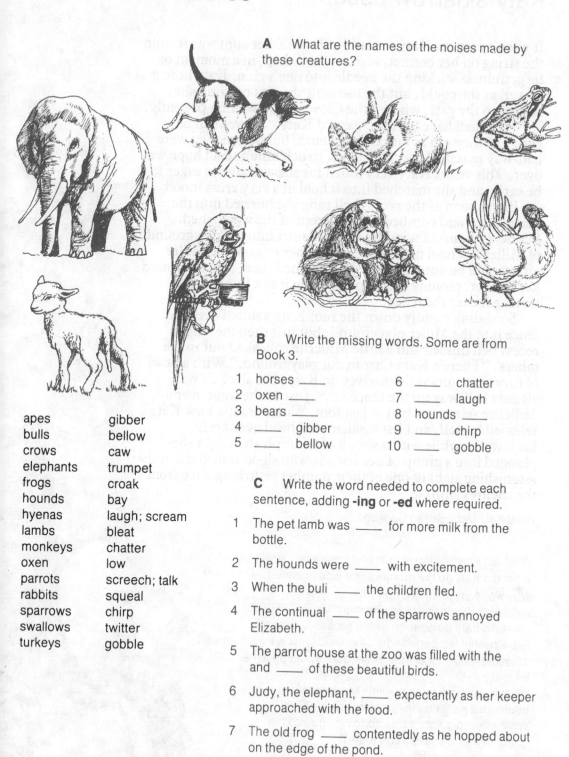

A What are the names of the noises made by these creatures?

apes   gibber
bulls   bellow
crows   caw
elephants   trumpet
frogs   croak
hounds   bay
hyenas   laugh; scream
lambs   bleat
monkeys   chatter
oxen   low
parrots   screech; talk
rabbits   squeal
sparrows   chirp
swallows   twitter
turkeys   gobble

B Write the missing words. Some are from Book 3.

1 horses _____
2 oxen _____
3 bears _____
4 _____ gibber
5 _____ bellow

6 _____ chatter
7 _____ laugh
8 hounds _____
9 _____ chirp
10 _____ gobble

C Write the word needed to complete each sentence, adding **-ing** or **-ed** where required.

1 The pet lamb was _____ for more milk from the bottle.

2 The hounds were _____ with excitement.

3 When the bull _____ the children fled.

4 The continual _____ of the sparrows annoyed Elizabeth.

5 The parrot house at the zoo was filled with the _____ and _____ of these beautiful birds.

6 Judy, the elephant, _____ expectantly as her keeper approached with the food.

7 The old frog _____ contentedly as he hopped about on the edge of the pond.

Katy's narrow escape

It wasn't easy for Katy to stand still while her aunt was sewing the string on her bonnet, and now and then, in a moment of forgetfulness sticking the needle into one's chin. Katy bore it as well as she could, but the moment she was released she rushed to the gate, where little Clover stood waiting patiently.

"We shall have to run," gasped Katy, "or we shall be late." So they ran as fast as they could, but before they were half-way to school the town clock struck nine and all hope was over. This vexed Katy very much for she was always eager to be early, and she marched into school in a very cross mood.

But as soon as the recess bell rang she hurried into the playground and climbed onto the roof of the wood-shed. Suddenly a gust of wind blew her bonnet into the playground of Miller's School next-door. In another minute the Miller girls would be out. Already she imagined them dancing round her bonnet, pinning it on a pole, using it as a football and waving it over the fence. . . .

So sliding rapidly down the roof Katy vaulted over the fence into the Miller playground, but just then the Miller recess bell tinkled and a little Millerite squeaked out to the others, "There's Katy Carr in our playground." With a howl of fury they hurled themselves on Katy, but she . . . was already half-way up the fence. . . . Just as she went over a Millerite seized her by the last foot. With a frantic kick Katy released herself, and her assailant fell head over heels backwards, while with a shriek of triumph and fright she plunged into a group of her friends who stood transfixed at the astonishing sight of one of their number returning alive from the enemy camp.

What Katy Did   Susan Coolidge

1   What did Katy's aunt do now and then when sewing the bonnet?
2   What did Katy do the moment she was released by her aunt?
3   Why was Katy in such a hurry?
4   What was Katy's mood as she marched into school?
5   What did Katy do as soon as the recess bell rang?
6   Explain what happened when the wind blew Katy's bonnet?
7   What did Katy imagine the Miller girls would do to her bonnet?
8   What happened when the little Millerite told the others that Katy was in their playground?
9   What effect did Katy's headlong plunge into her group of friends have upon them?

Sounds

Object	Sound
anvil	clang
bagpipes	skirl
bell	peal; tinkle
bow	twang
brakes	grinding
bullet	ping
chains	jangle; rattle
coins	clink; jingle
corks	pop
dishes	rattle; clatter
engine	throb
explosion	blast
hinges	creak
rifle	report
silk	rustle
siren	wail
skirts	swish
stream	babble; murmur
thunder	clap; peal
wings	whirr

A Write the missing words; some you learnt in Books 2 and 3.

1 the twang of a ____
2 the call of a ____
3 the tinkle of a ____
4 the jingle of ____
5 the shuffle of ____
6 the rustle of ____
7 the grinding of ____
8 the babble of a ____
9 the lash of a ____
10 the skirl of ____
11 the ____ of skirts
12 the ____ of dishes
13 the ____ of corks
14 the ____ of a bullet
15 the ____ of hoofs
16 the ____ of raindrops
17 the ____ of a rifle
18 the ____ of chains
19 the ____ of an anvil
20 a ____ of thunder

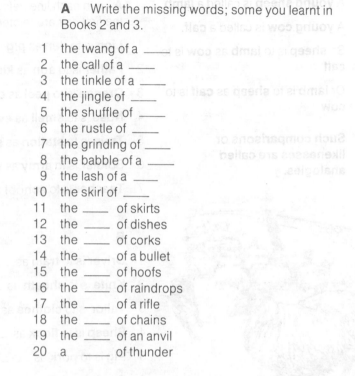

B Write in order the words necessary to complete these sentences.

1 With a noisy ____ of wings thousands of starlings descended on the town.

2 The bridal pair left the church to the merry ____ of bells.

3 The workmen were temporarily deafened by the ____ of the explosion.

4 The frequent ____ of the anvil showed how busy the blacksmith was.

5 When hinges ____ they require oiling.

6 The ____ of the siren announced that a fire had broken out.

7 The Highland regiment marched to the ____ of bagpipes.

8 Derek tossed restlessly in his bunk, disturbed by the ____ of the ship's engines.

Analogies

A **young sheep** is called a **lamb**.

A **young cow** is called a **calf**.

So **sheep** is to **lamb** as **cow** is to **calf**.

Or **lamb** is to **sheep** as **calf** is to **cow**.

Such comparisons or likenesses are called analogies.

A   In each line below, consider how the words in the first pair are related, then write the missing word.

1   **Lion** is to **den** as **pig** is to ____ .

2   **Father** is to **son** as **king** is to ____ .

3   **Orange** is to **peel** as **cheese** is to ____ .

4   **Nose** is to **smell** as **eye** is to ____ .

5   **Train** is to **station** as **ship** is to ____ .

6   **Soldier** is to **army** as **sailor** is to ____ .

7   **Teacher** is to **school** as **nurse** is to ____ .

B

1   **Driver** is to **train** as ____ is to **plane**.

2   **Knife** is to **sheath** as ____ is to **scabbard**.

3   **Tailor** is to **clothes** as ____ is to **bread**.

4   **Sheep** is to **flock** as ____ is to **pack**.

5   **Pig** is to **pork** as ____ is to **venison**.

6   **Famine** is to **food** as ____ is to **water**.

7   **Dog** is to **bark** as ____ is to **trumpet**.

C   There is another way of writing these analogies.
sheep : lamb :: cow : calf

1   **bank : manager :: school :**

2   **hand : palm :: foot :**

3   **teacher : pupil :: doctor :**

4   **bird : air :: fish :**

5   **bee : insect :: snake**

6   **husband : wife :: earl :**

7   **house : floor :: ship**

Doers of actions

Action	Doer
apply	applicant
auction	auctioneer
burgle	burglar
capture	captor
challenge	challenger
compete	competitor
contribute	contributor
correspond	correspondent
criticize	critic
dictate	dictator
edit	editor
guard	guardian
lie	liar
mutiny	mutineer
operate	operator
oppose	opponent
preside	president
represent	representative
succeed	successor
survive	survivor

Memorize this list, then answer the questions.

A What word is used for:

1 one who challenges?
2 one who contributes?
3 one who edits?
4 one who presides?
5 one who lies?
6 one who criticizes?
7 one who applies?
8 one who operates?
9 one who competes?
10 one who survives?

B Complete each sentence by inserting the word for the doer of the action.

1 A ___ broke into the bank last night.   **burgle**

2 The young orphan was accompanied by his ___ .   **guard**

3 In two hours the ___ had sold all the paintings.   **auction**

4 One ___ was shot in the chest.   **mutiny**

5 The prisoner was treated well by his ___ .   **capture**

6 A ___ of the company called to demonstrate their automatic washing machine.   **represent**

7 Some countries do not have a monarch or a president; they have a ___ .   **dictate**

8 In less than a minute the wrestler had thrown his ___ .   **oppose**

9 The retiring caretaker showed his ___ round the school.   **succeed**

10 The film star ordered a photograph to be sent to every ___ .   **correspond**

Twin words

Learn this list of **twin words** before answering the questions which follow. Exercise B shows how these expressions are used.

bag and baggage
beck and call
body and soul
fame and fortune
fire and water
hale and hearty
hue and cry
neck and neck
rack and ruin
rough and ready
sixes and sevens
spick and span

A Copy these expressions and insert the missing words.

1 fame and ____
2 ____ and ready
3 hale and ____
4 ____ and neck
5 beck and ____
6 ____ and sevens
7 body and ____
8 ____ and ruin
9 fire and ____
10 ____ and span
11 bag and ____
12 ____ and cry

B What are the words omitted from these sentences?

1 Everything at the little hotel was very rough and ____ .

2 For the last fifty metres the two horses were running neck and ____ .

3 The poor widow's pension was barely enough to keep ____ and soul together.

4 The pageboy was at everybody's ____ and call.

5 There was a ____ and cry as the pickpocket fled down the street, followed by a big crowd.

6 The dishonest lodger was put out ____ and baggage.

7 A man will go through ____ and water for the woman he loves.

8 Unfortunately the beautiful old mansion had been allowed to go to rack and ____ .

9 A spick and ____ room is spotlessly clean and very neat and tidy.

10 Many a Briton has decided to seek ____ and fortune in Australia.

Rhymes

in
kin
admire
attire
thin
pin
bigger
figure
head
red
skin
chin

A   Write the words, numbered from 1 to 12, which fill the spaces in this extract from a poem.

"Come in," the Mayor cried, looking ___ : 1
And in did come the strangest ___ ! 2
His queer long coat from heel to ___ , 3
Was half of yellow and half of ___ , 4
And he himself was tall and ___ , 5
With sharp blue eyes, each like a ___ , 6
And light loose hair, yet swarthy ___ , 7
No tuft on cheek, nor beard on ___ , 8
But lips where smiles went out and ___ ; 9
There was no guessing his kith and ___ 10
And nobody could enough ___ 11
The tall man and his quaint ___ . 12

B   Each of these lines contains three rhyming words from which some of the letters are missing. Complete each word.

Example   1   work
                     jerk
                     shirk

1 work   2 home   3 grows
   j ___ _   f ___   ch ___ _
   sh ___ _   c ___   fr ___ _

4 course   5 become   6 stole
   f ___ _ _   cr ___ _   sh ___ _
   h ___ _ _ _   gl ___   scr ___ _ _

7 nurse   8 cheer   9 bought
   v ___ _ _   sm ___ _   c ___ _ _ _
   w ___ _ _   sph ___ _   t ___ _

C   Write as eight lines of poetry:

I have a garden of my own, shining with flowers of every hue; I loved it dearly while alone, but I shall love it more with you: and there the golden bees shall come in summer-time at break of morn, and wake us with their busy hum, around the Silea's fragrant thorn.

A fight in a signal-tower

Up over the edge of the spur, three wild horsemen appeared heading for the gateway.

As they dropped from their ponies in the courtyard below, Marcus and Esca drew back from the parapet. "Only three, so far," Marcus whispered. "Don't use your knife unless you have to. They may be of more use to us living than dead."

Esca nodded, and returned his hunting-knife to his belt. Life and the urgency of doing had taken hold of them again. Flattened against the wall on either side of the stairhead they waited, listening to their pursuers questing through storehouse and guardroom. "Fools!" Marcus breathed, as a shout told them that the stairway had been spotted; and then came a rush of feet that checked at the floor below and then came on, storming upward.

Marcus was a good boxer, and much practice with the cestus last winter had made Esca something of a boxer also; together, weary though they were, they made a dangerous team. The first two tribesmen to come ducking out through the low doorway went down without a sound, like poled oxen; the third, not so completely caught unawares, put up more of a fight. Esca flung himself upon him, and they crashed down several steps together, in a flailing mass of arms and legs. There was a short, desperate struggle before Esca came uppermost, and staggering clear, heaved an unconscious man over the doorsill.

The Eagle of the Ninth Rosemary Sutcliff

1 Where were Marcus and Esca when the horsemen appeared?
2 Where did the horsemen dismount?
3 Which words suggest there might have been more horsemen to come?
4 Why did Marcus advise Esca not to use his knife?
5 Where did Esca keep his knife?
6 Where were their pursuers searching for them?
7 Why did Marcus describe their pursuers as fools?
8 What kind of training had made Esca into a boxer?
9 Why did the third tribesman put up more of a fight than the other two?
10 In what state was the third tribesman after the fight?

Double negatives

Words containing **not** or **no** are called **negatives**.

Examples
no not nobody nothing
nowhere none never (*not ever*)

Two negatives should never be used together in the same sentence.

Wrong
He did **not** tell me **nothing** about it. (*two negatives*)

Right
He did **not** tell me anything about it. (*one negative*)

He told me **nothing** about it. (*one negative*)

Choose the correct word from the pair above to complete each sentence.

1 **nothing   anything**
John did not tell his father ____ about the accident.
John told his father ____ about the accident.

2 **nowhere   anywhere**
We couldn't find the book ____ .
The book was ____ to be found.

3 **nothing   anything**
The gardener didn't pay Tom ____ for his help.
The gardener paid Tom ____ for his help.

4 **never   ever**
Don't you ____ get tired of knitting?
Do you ____ get tired of knitting?

5 **nothing   anything**
We could not see ____ from where we stood.
We could see ____ from where we stood.

6 **no   any**
There isn't ____ cake left.
There is ____ cake left.

7 **nobody   anybody**
We didn't meet ____ on the way home.
We met ____ on the way home.

8 **no   any**
Haven't you ____ sympathy for him?
Have you ____ sympathy for him?

9 **none   any**
I asked Bill for a sweet but he didn't have ____ .
I asked Bill for a sweet but he had ____ .

10 **no one   anyone**
We can't find ____ to dig our garden.
We can find ____ to dig our garden.

11 **nothing   anything**
There isn't ____ wrong with this car.
There is ____ wrong with this car.

12 **no   any**
I looked everywhere but couldn't find ____ bluebells.
I looked everywhere but could find ____ bluebells.

Proverbs

Learn these proverbs and their meanings well before attempting the questions.

Charity begins at home.	Be kind to relatives before showing kindness to strangers.
What's sauce for the goose is sauce for the gander	One person should be entitled to the same treatment as another.
It is never too late to mend	However old a person is it is not too late for him to reform.
Every cloud has a silver lining	However dark the present may seem the future holds something brighter.
A bird in the hand is worth two in the bush	It is wiser to accept an offer now than to depend on a better offer you may have in the future.

A

1 What has every cloud got?

2 Where does charity begin?

3 What do barking dogs seldom do?

4 What is worth two birds in the bush?

B Complete these proverbs. Give the meanings of Nos. 2, 3, 5, 8 and 9.

1 A friend in need . . .

2 Strike while the . . .

3 Charity begins . . .

4 What's sauce for the goose . . .

5 A bird in the hand . . .

6 Every cloud . . .

7 It is never too late . . .

8 A stitch in time . . .

9 A rolling stone . . .

10 Necessity is the . . .

11 Look before you . . .

Similes

Learn this list of **similes** thoroughly before attempting the exercises.

as blind as a bat
as dry as dust
as frisky as a lamb
as large as life
as pale as death
as sound as a bell
as tender as a chicken
as thick as thieves
as timid as a mouse
as tough as leather

Complete these similes.

A

1 as pale as ____
2 as dry as ____
3 as blind as a ____
4 as thick as ____
5 as frisky as a ____
6 as ____ as a bell
7 as ____ as a chicken
8 as ____ as a mouse
9 as ____ as leather
10 as ____ as life

B Revision

1 as meek as a ____
2 as pleased as ____
3 as patient as ____
4 as slippery as an ____
5 as smooth as ____
6 as ____ as a new pin
7 as ____ as a button
8 as ____ as brass
9 as ____ as sugar
10 as ____ as a fiddle

C Write the words which have been omitted from these sentences.

1 The two women in the wrecked car were as pale as ____ .

2 The little girl is as timid as a ____ .

3 One guest at the guest house complained that the beef was as tough as ____ .

4 The new puppy was as frisky as a ____ .

5 The two boys were as thick as ____ .

6 The old gentleman is getting as blind as a ____ .

7 In walked Mr. Micawber, as large as ____ .

8 After being repaired the toy was as sound as a ____ .

9 Sheila found the book as dry as ____ .

10 Alan woke up feeling as ____ as a button.

Fun with words

By rearranging some of the letters in the word
separate
we can make other words.

Examples   spear
             spare
             pears
             rates
             stare
             steep etc.

A   In the same way, use the letters of the word in bold type below to form words to complete the sentences which follow.

consecrated

1   The _ _ _ _ _ Tom threw broke the kitchen window.

2   A church is a very_ _ _ _ _ _ building.

3   When you _ _ _ _ _ at something you look at it with a fixed gaze.

4   The Fairy Queen was _ _ _ _ _ _ on her throne.

5   A horse is sometimes called a _ _ _ _ _ .

6   A male honey-bee is called a _ _ _ _ _ _ .

7   A _ _ _ _ _ _ is something you do not wish others to know.

B   Write the six words in the list below which cannot be formed from the letters in the word:

comparative

1 private	7 carton	13 compare
2 cramp	8 vicar	14 repair
3 create	9 crêpe	15 taper
4 viper	10 prove	16 voter
5 price	11 carrot	17 treat
6 cream	12 crate	18 impart

C   In each line find the word which corresponds to one of the given meanings. By rearranging the letters of this word you have the word which matches the other meaning.

1   the staff of life;
    hair on the face

2   the backbone;
    evergreen trees with needle-shaped leaves

3   a room where butter is made;
    a record of daily happenings

4   another word for "wept";
    a drink made from the juice of apples

Idioms

Learn this list of idioms and their meanings, then work the test which follows.

Idiom	Meaning
to send to Coventry	to ignore a person
to play second fiddle	to take a back place while someone else leads
to take French leave	to go off without permission
to be at loggerheads	to be quarrelling
to make a mountain out of a molehill	to make trifling difficulties appear great ones
to feather one's nest	to increase one's possessions
to pay through the nose	to pay too high a price
to smell a rat	to be suspicious
to give a person the cold shoulder	to make him feel unwelcome
to blow one's own trumpet	to boast about oneself

Rewrite these sentences substituting for the words in bold type one of the **idioms** in the list.

1   Robinson paid **far too high a price** for his house.

2   It is wrong to think only of **adding to one's possessions**.

3   Some people prefer **to take a back place and let someone else take the lead**.

4   Very soon the police began **to be suspicious**.

5   Alan is too fond of **boasting about himself**.

6   The two neighbours are forever **quarrelling**.

7   Faint-hearted people often like making **difficulties appear much greater than they really are**.

8   The blackleg's mates **ignored him and refused to talk to him**.

9   The soldier took **the week-end off without the permission of his commanding officer**.

10 The old couple decided to give the tramp **the impression that he was most unwelcome**.

89

Long John Silver

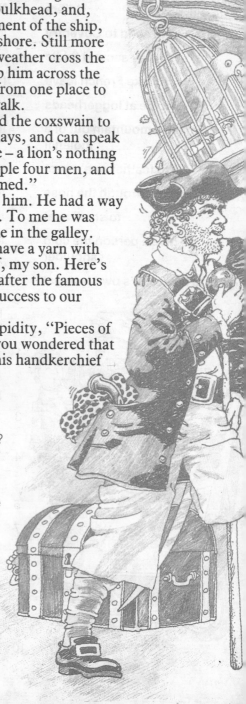

Long John Silver, our ship's cook – Barbecue, as the men called him – carried his crutch by a lanyard round his neck, to have both hands as free as possible. It was something to see him wedge the foot of his crutch against a bulkhead, and, propped against it, yielding to every movement of the ship, get on with his cooking like someone safe ashore. Still more strange was it to see him in the heaviest of weather cross the deck. He had a line or two rigged up to help him across the widest spaces, and he would hand himself from one place to another, as quickly as another man could walk.

"He's no common man, Barbecue," said the coxswain to me. "He had good schooling in his young days, and can speak like a book when so minded, and he's brave – a lion's nothing alongside of Long John! I've seen him grapple four men, and knock their heads together – and him unarmed."

All the crew respected and even obeyed him. He had a way of doing everybody some particular service. To me he was unweariedly kind; and always glad to see me in the galley.

"Hawkins," he would say, "come and have a yarn with John. Nobody more welcome than yourself, my son. Here's Cap'n Flint – I calls my parrot Cap'n Flint after the famous buccaneer – here's Cap'n Flint predicting success to our voyage. Wasn't you, cap'n?"

And the parrot would say, with great rapidity, "Pieces of eight! pieces of eight! pieces of eight!" till you wondered that it was not out of breath, or till John threw his handkerchief over the cage.

Treasure Island   Robert Louis Stevenson

1   What nickname did the crew give Long John Silver?
2   How did John carry his crutch?
3   Why did he carry it in this way?
4   How did he use his crutch when cooking?
5   What helped John to cross the widest spaces of the deck in the heaviest weather?
6   What example of John's bravery did the coxswain give?
7   Why did the crew respect John?
8   What was the name of John's parrot?
9   After whom was he named?
10 How did John stop the parrot talking?